WOMEN WHO RUN

D0961689

WOMEN
WHO RUN

by Shanti Sosienski

Seal Press

Women Who Run

Copyright © 2006 Shanti Sosienski

Published by Seal Press
1400 65th Street, Suite 250
Emeryville, CA 94608

All rights reserved. No part of this book may be reproduced or transmitted in any form without written permission from the publisher, except by reviewers who may quote brief excerpts in connection with a review.

9 8 7 6 5 4
Library of Congress Cataloging-in-Publication Data

Sosienski, Shanti.
Women who run / Shanti Sosienski.
p. cm.
ISBN-13: 978-1-58005-183-5
ISBN-10: 1-58005-183-9
1. Women runners—Case studies. I. Title.

GV1061.10.W66S67 2006
796.42082—dc22
2006005460

Cover design by Gerilyn Attebery
Interior design by Elise Winter
Printed in Canada by Transcontinental

Dedication

To my grandmother, Eleanor Sosienski, who played tennis until she was eighty and only quit when she got knocked out by a fastball one afternoon. And to Rebecca Rusch, who taught me that the body and mind are capable of so much more than we ever could imagine. And lastly, to all of the women in my life, especially my mom, who have inspired me to run hard, run fast, and live fully because life only has the limits I put on it.

Contents

Introduction: Why I Run

Until I was thirty-four, I never thought of myself as a runner. There were times when I called myself a snowboarder, a surfer, a mountain biker. I just started rock-climbing, and I occasionally paraglide. I often go in-line skating on the boardwalk that connects Santa Monica to Venice Beach.

But I was never a runner. This is funny, considering I grew up in Eugene, Oregon, the capital of running, the home of legendary University of Oregon runner Steve Prefontaine, who died at age twenty-four in a car accident before he hit his prime; Olympian Mary Decker Slaney, who set four world records in the 1980s for distances from eight hundred yards to two miles; and three-time New York marathon winner Alberto Salazar. I grew up ten blocks from the university's Hayward field, where famed track coaches Bill Bowerman and Phil Knight tested homemade rubber waffle-soled shoes on the U of O track team in the late '60s. In 1986, when I was fifteen, I waited tables downstairs from one of the first Nike stores, in the Fifth Street Public Market, in downtown Eugene. I remember coveting the wall of Nikes on my lunch break, wishing I had $70 to sink into a pair—but only because I thought they looked cool. I was still years away from my first running experience.

□ □ □

Fast-forward to a day in early March 2005. It was my second trip to Thailand, a few months after the devastating tsunami of December 26, 2004, which I narrowly avoided. During my first trip in December, my mom, my sister, and I were on Koh Lanta and Koh Phi Phi, two of the islands in Thailand that were hit by the massive waves. I got on a plane on the evening of December 25. Sitting in Bangkok the next day, I remember feeling lucky to be alive.

When I returned home to Los Angeles in December, I was determined to go back and find the people I met during my trip. I wanted to help them rebuild their lives. The first few months of the year were spent deeply entrenched in fundraising on behalf of the tsunami survivors, mostly ignoring my career and my husband of five months. We had grown estranged, and by March, it was clear we were breaking up. I felt like I had a metaphorical tsunami in my life, wiping away everything in my world I thought I was sure about.

When I returned to Thailand, my first stop was Phuket. I stayed with Neil and Tik Satterwhite, an American-Thai couple I met through various friends who ran a hotel on Kata Beach called Tik's Place. They were raising money for children who had lost family and for people who had lost homes and businesses in the tsunami.

Neil's energy was astounding. He certainly didn't look sixty years old—or like the father of a daughter my age. When I asked him his secret, he simply said, "I run." Every morning, Neil got up and ran six times back and forth on a nearly mile-long beach. He rarely missed a morning. The next day, I got up early, put on my running shoes, and joined him on the beach. He had packed a small cooler with water and one beer, a reward after we finished the run. Kata is like many of the beaches in Thailand. The water is aquamarine, the sky is usually cloudless, and the sun is hot—even early in the morning. I ran with Neil for maybe half of the length of the beach but quickly got winded.

As I trudged along, out of breath, I liked what I felt—and I hated it at the same time. My body was jiggling from too many years of not much exercise and much sitting at my desk. I felt alert though, and alive in a way I hadn't in the months leading up my ex-husband's confession to having an affair and the horror of the tsunami. Running felt hard, but it also felt good. Somehow I forgot that all of my life I had hated running. In fact, I hated it so much that I was kicked off the soccer team during my junior year in high school because the coach wanted me to run and I refused.

So what happened? Looking back, I think I was ready for the challenge, the sense of accomplishment, the endorphin rush, and the distraction that running provided during a particularly hard time in my life. That day in Thailand, I felt like a runner. I only completed one and a half miles, but it felt good. I sat on the beach and stretched while I waited for Neil as he completed his additional four and a half miles.

"Feels pretty good, huh?" he asked me when he had finished his run, offering me the water and cracking a beer for himself.

The next day, I ran again and completed two miles. Then, on the third day, Neil had to make a business trip to Bangkok, so I ran alone, completing almost three miles (walking a good part of it so I could go further). Then I ran the next day. Every day, I passed a woman who was obviously a serious runner. Her body was tan and toned, and she would still be running when I was finished. I could leave the beach after my short runs, go back to my hotel, get my bathing suit and beach gear, come back—and she would still be running. I remember wondering what made her stick with it. What did she think about? How far did she run? How did she get started running? Would I ever run like her, or would I just get tired of it after a couple of weeks?

I didn't get tired of it. When I returned home, running was my therapy. If I was angry or sad or just frustrated with anything, I would go running. This meant there were days when I would sit in my running clothes all day and every few hours go out for another run. At first it was just a few blocks of running and a lot of walking, but slowly I found I could run more blocks, then more blocks, faster. Eventually I got a slick little blue Timex marathon watch and started recording my times here and there. It was exciting to watch my time come down. One day I ran a mile in thirteen minutes, and then a week later, it was twelve minutes.

I didn't necessarily feel stronger with every run. On some runs, I felt weak. It was during these runs that I learned to dig deep and keep going even though I was bored, disappointed with my run, not really feeling like it. As I began talking to other women who ran, I realized they experienced the same thing and that not every run is perfect, that there are times when you just don't feel like putting on your shoes. But once you do, and you get out there, your body starts to remember the rhythm, the feeling that running gives you, the feeling that you know: This is what you should be doing, and this is what your body needs.

Even though it was a real challenge, I ran almost every day through the spring and into the early summer. My iPod relieved some of the boredom I felt at first, but eventually I started finding better, more contemplative ways to entertain myself. I would run different routes to the park at the end of my street. I would make up various reasons why the palms on Sixth Street seemed to bend toward the east unlike the palms on other streets. Even on days when my inclination on every other step was to stop, for some reason, I kept running. I felt the tension from the previous weeks draining out of my body, and as I ran I looked around at my neighborhood. I was surprised at how quiet the area was for an afternoon, and how few cars drove by.

I can distinctly remember the night I started to really love running. It was one of those perfect warm Southern California evenings, when the sky is pink and the sun is setting slowly over the ocean. At that point, I still had many days when I felt like a weak runner, but at the same time, I had also started to understand what it felt like when the endorphins coursed through my body. That night, I thought about how it had only been a few weeks earlier when I lasted maybe thirty minutes, and how now I could run for an hour. As I ran along the coast, I felt myself smiling as I relaxed into my run.

In June 2005, I went to Sun Valley, Idaho, to stay with my friend and athletic mentor, Rebecca Rusch, for six weeks. In the mountains surrounding Sun Valley, I started to learn how to relax my body while running and to get into that almost meditative state. I still marveled every time I ran at how it made me feel, whether I ran fifteen minutes or two hours. It was still hard to believe I was actually running and enjoying it. I was fascinated by the fact that my body felt strong some days, like a finely tuned machine, and pathetic other days. Either way, it put me in touch with my physical self, from my breath to the bottoms of my feet. Running taught me how to look inward, to calm down, to find *jai yen yen,* or "a cool heart," as they say in Thailand. With every step, it pushed me through anger and weakness, through sadness and disappointment. On some runs I would find myself crying, and other runs would make me laugh as I looked up at green mountains or across a fragrant field of purple and white wildflowers. Running had brought me to these beautiful places, and strangely enough, it had become a dependable friend.

Later that summer, I was asked to write a book about women who run. Over the course of interviewing women for this book, I met those who run for fun, for fitness, for fame, for stamina both physical and mental, because they want to meet people, because they want to change the world. With each woman, I learned something new about running and something new about myself.

Writing this book was a project that began as a marathon and soon became an ultra run. There were so many more miles to go, so many more women to talk to, but eventually I had to accept that the end was in sight and work toward it. One woman I interviewed but never met was Helen Klein. At eighty-four, she has run 143 ultras (defined as runs over 50 miles) and 70 marathons—and she didn't start running until she was fifty-five. Helen first went running with her husband, Norm, who was challenged by a friend to do a ten-mile race. She told me she couldn't imagine running that far at the time, but once they ran the race, they loved it so much that they sold all of their belongings and moved from the Midwest to Sacramento, California, to train for more runs. Helen's husband became the organizer for the famously grueling Western States, an ultra run of one hundred miles in the Sierra Nevada, which Helen has completed many times.

What is Helen's secret at eighty-four? Other than good genetics, she swears by her daily routine: Wake up at 4:00 AM, eat a piece of fresh-baked bread with almond butter and bananas, go for a two-hour run. "Because of my running, I have been able to see a lot of things I wouldn't have been able to see otherwise," Helen told me. "We ran up to 17,000 feet in Peru. I ran in Africa in Marathon des Sables. That was 143 miles across the desert this last summer. I've been on humanitarian missions to Nepal and Ethiopia. We put on races for the Ethiopian children for four days. They ran like the wind. They ran in their bare feet."

As Helen discovered and as I have now found, running becomes part of your soul once you find it. It's like that for so many people. Long runs or short runs, up or downhill, pavement or trails, competitive or not. It's addictive and it's soothing, but more than anything, it reminds us how alive we are.

As of this writing, I have only pinned a race number on myself once, for a fun 5K run called the Wasatch Wobble, in Salt Lake City in August 2005. Even though it wasn't a serious race and there were no prizes, it was exciting to run in a pack—watching people pass me, and passing people myself. I ran for a while with one woman who worked for the ski and snowboard company Salomon; I had met her the previous day at the trade show. She and I bonded on that trail run through a park in Salt Lake City without words. I followed her lead for a good half of the race, and then she dropped me, but it was still fun to run with her in companionable silence. At the finish line, my friend Rebecca—who, being a professional athlete, had led the race—cheered us all in. It was so exciting to cross the finish line, for nothing more than just knowing I completed a 5K.

Running has since taken on a different meaning for me: It isn't about losing weight or dealing with my emotions, it is about dedicating myself to training and believing that I am up to the challenge. I—a woman who has disdained running for so long—now believe in it like a religion, and I now dream of running a marathon.

It's only a matter of time.

□ □ □

In late October of 2005 I moved to Ketchum, Idaho, after living in Southern California for six years. Ketchum is the mountain town that sits below Sun Valley resort. As winter set in, I faced new running challenges. I had to learn to run in snow and to motivate myself on cold days, which wasn't easy. One day, I slipped on black ice and went down—hard. As I lay there for a second, my head spinning, I couldn't help but laugh at my city-girl ignorance. Getting used to Idaho was going to take some time, but it would happen.

After two weeks in Idaho, I missed my friend Devin, who lived in California. Shortly after I returned from Thailand, she became my first and only running partner. She was also a magazine writer and was just finishing her first book, so almost every day, we would call each other and set a time to go running. Sometimes we walked, sometimes we ran, sometimes we huffed our way up and down a set of stairs near my house. Meanwhile, I learned about her life, about how she was a "fat kid" growing up and lost fifty-five pounds thanks to running. Whenever I ran with Devin, I liked how it never felt competitive. Some days she was stronger, and other days I took the lead. Either way, we stuck it out together and pushed each other on those days when we would have rather gone out for happy hour cocktails.

During that time, I shared thoughts with Devin that I didn't feel comfortable about sharing with anyone else. I didn't know whether it was the running that brought out that honesty, and it didn't really matter. All I knew was that in Idaho, I missed her, because there are times when it's just nice to have someone to encourage you to run further when you might not have enough energy on your own.

Before I left California, I learned about another group of women who ran together—a running club called the Janes. They are a group of elite women runners who meet in Santa Monica near the beach every Tuesday night to train. They are all former high school and college track stars, and they still run competitively. One woman, Erika Akulfi, was a triathlete who recently went professional. She led the pack as they set off running east up San Vicente, a residential tree-lined street. I wished I could run with them, but they were too fast for me. Instead I followed alongside in a car with their coach,

Tania Fisher, who was also a member of The Janes but was pregnant and therefore taking a breather from running.

I remembered how the women paced each other. Erika led the pack by nearly half a block at times. Her lean body moved effortlessly as she pumped her arms and stared straight ahead. They were doing intervals. When they came to a rest point, where they jogged instead of running at full power, Erika slowed down so she could run with her friends. It was exciting watching them run. It was also wonderful to see how they hugged each other after runs, that they had such a tight bond in spite of obvious differences.

The Janes run together because it motivates them and helps them judge how well they are doing. To these women, competition isn't a dirty word. It makes them stronger.

□ □ □

The women who fill the pages of this book run to keep from getting caught up in the monotony of life. They run because it helps break up the day-to-day—because even if they run the same path every day, no two runs are ever alike. One day you are strong, the next you are weak, and the next day you are ready to take on the world, because you solved everything midway through a run.

Running for these women is the place where they draw their inspiration to be mothers, wives, friends, leaders, rebels. Running is also the one place where there is no right or wrong, no rules, no time limits, no discrimination. Today, women can run almost anywhere, and they do—from the Sahara Desert and Tibet to the top of Mt. Tamalpais in Marin County, California. And while there are still limits in other parts of the world for women, and a notion in some places that running spoils a woman's purity (as runner Asra Nomani experienced in Pakistan), many run anyway, or are willing to face the consequences of trying.

When I think about what it would be like to be forbidden to run, I think about a girl named Weda whom I met three years ago when teaching a writing class to teenagers from conflict zones around the world. There were Muslim girls from Pakistan and Afghanistan sitting next to Jews from Israel. There was a girl from Cyprus and another from the Gaza Strip. Weda was a quiet seventeen-year-old from Kabul who spoke limited English. On the first day, when we introduced ourselves to each other, she told our group that she had been engaged to a man with "the gray hairs" when she was thirteen in an arranged marriage, which she was eventually able to escape. She also told us that she dreamed of running one day. She loved how it felt to have the wind in her hair and to run without a burqa constricting her movement.

At the end of the class one afternoon, I pulled Weda aside and offered to buy her a new pair of running shoes because I knew she was poor. She smiled sweetly and thanked me, then refused the offer, saying, "This is kind of you, but what would I do with running shoes? I have nowhere to run." In the war-torn city where she lives, if a woman were to try to run on the streets, it would be a sign of something wrong, and she would either be arrested or men would think her immodest and inappropriate. She could be jailed or even worse for her rebelliousness. "Women don't run where I come from. But someday I will make it so women can run," she told me.

It's hard to imagine women not being allowed to perform such a natural act as running, but this was the case in April 2005 in Pakistan, when fifty women were arrested for attempting to run in a public marathon that was supposedly open for women. And as I wrote this book, I was surprised to learn that it has only been thirty-five years since women could legally run in marathons in the United States. Prior to that, women were physically pulled out of races by organizers when they ran alongside their male friends. There was no marathon event for women in the Olympics until 1984, and it wasn't until 1996 that the 5,000-meter and 10,000-meter events were included on the program for women.

□ □ □

Yesterday, I went running. It was a short run, about two miles, on a bike path leading out of Ketchum. The sun was out, the path was mostly cleared, the air was crisp. It was a fast day for me, and I felt strong. When I have days like that, I wonder why I don't run twice a day, every day. Running becomes something else, deeper and more ingrained in your body, once you are hooked. And for those who have ever felt that running high, whether it was last week or in high school, they talk about it fondly, with a dreamy look in their eye. They can recount that feeling of running and will agree that there are few other sports that leave you feeling so free.

Each one of the women in these pages knows that feeling of freedom. They share a passion for running that unites them in sisterhood. And while some of them were born for running, others weren't, and had to teach themselves to love it. It's such a simple thing, to put one foot in front of the other, but it has changed all of their lives, and mine as well.

So enjoy reading, but feel free to put the book down and go for a run. None of us will blame you or take it personally. We're right there with you.

Shanti Sosienski
Ketchum, Idaho
June 2006

Chapter One: Marathon Women

It's hard to believe now, but just forty years ago, women weren't allowed to run long-distance races. In 2005, of the 383,000 people who finished marathons around the country, 40 percent were women. Until 1960, the longest Olympic event for women's running was a mere two hundred meters. Now women like Olympian Paula Radcliffe have world record marathon times that are sub-2:20—that's more than two hours faster than the first woman known to run a marathon in Greece in 1896.

But whether or not the International Olympic Committee has recognized it, women have always found a way to run. The history of women's competitive racing can be traced back to ancient Greece, when every five years a short footrace was held at a women's festival to honor the Greek goddess Hera. In 1896, a woman named Stamatis Rovithi was said to have run the proposed marathon course in Athens a month before the Olympics. The next month, when the Games were held, another woman, Melpomene, tried to enter the Olympics for the marathon and was denied because of her gender. She ran alongside the men anyway and arrived at the stadium an hour and a half after the winner, with a time of 4:30.

Women had their own separate form of Olympics in 1922 and 1926, as well as their own international federation—the Federation Sportive Feminine Internationale. In 1928, fed up with being excluded from the regular Olympics, they negotiated with the International Olympic Committee and were granted an experimental program of five events, one of which was the 800 meters. The catch was that in exchange they would have to hand over the control of their federation and their championships. Hopeful to make progress in the world of women's sports, they agreed. But women at that time didn't know how to train for long distances, so during the 800-meter race in the 1928 Olympics, several women collapsed, and as a result, the event was dropped.

The early running pioneers had sacrificed their independence and control to be a part of the men's Olympic track and field program, and the world of women's sports took a blow because of it. During and after the Great Depression, the idea of women being athletes had been squashed. America went into a conservative period, and competition among women was frowned upon. It was not until the late '60s that women began to fight to play competitive sports and run longer distances. In 1960, a full thirty-two years later, the 800-meter race reappeared in the Olympics for women; until then, nothing over 200 meters was allowed. The next step was the addition of the 1,500-meter race in 1972.

In 1983, after an ACLU lawsuit was filed against the Olympic Committee on behalf of women distance runners, the 5,000- and 10,000-meter events were added. And finally, in 1984—almost a hundred years after Melpomene and Stamatis Rovithi ran 26.2 miles on the sly in Athens—other women could boldly say they had run an Olympic marathon.

Between 1966—when Bobbi Gibb became the first woman to (unofficially) run the Boston Marathon—and 1984, when Joan Benoit Samuelson (officially) won the first Olympic women's marathon—the number of women runners flourished. Some of them fought the corporate side of getting women into marathons and the Olympics, while others fought it out in the trenches, running their hearts out and setting world records.

When it comes to distance running, the Boston Marathon is one of the oldest and most prestigious marathons in North America, dating back to its first race in 1896. In the early '60s, the race was one of the premier events in the running world, and with all the attention it was receiving, it was easy for it to become a staging ground for revolution in women's distance running. Through running in the Boston Marathon, three women in particular—Bobbi Gibb, Kathrine Switzer, and Jacqueline Hansen—forever changed the course of women's distance running, each in her own way.

□ □ □

Roberta "Bobbi" Gibb grew up in the suburbs of Boston in the '40s and '50s. In high school there was no such thing as track and field for girls. She could play field hockey or tennis, but in general, when girls became women, running was not supposed to be part of their existence. It wasn't ladylike.

Bobbi loved being outdoors. She went horseback riding in the summers and raced around her neighborhood the rest of the year, challenging the boys and girls on her block to sprints. She was fast and knew it. "I had always been active," she says. "When I was growing up, if I saw a green grassy field, I had this upwelling sense of joy. I would run across it with my arms up in the air. I couldn't help myself. It was a love of life."

In high school she spent many afternoons running the wooded trails near her home. Her love for running didn't come from a strong sense of competition. It was a simple love of nature, of being alone, of feeling her body move. In fact she had no idea that marathons even existed until she heard about the Boston Marathon from her best friend's father in 1964, around the time she was entering college. At the time the race was just a few hundred men who belonged to the Boston Athletic Club; they would run 26.2 miles around Boston on what is now the official Boston Marathon course. Bobbi and her dad went to watch the race that year, and she soon decided she wanted to run in it.

"Here were people running on the earth, and they had such a sense of themselves as they ran through Boston," says Bobbi. "I could see it in their faces. I just decided I was going to run the race. It wasn't for prize money. I didn't even realize at that point women weren't allowed to run."

At that time, Bobbi had a boyfriend who used to run 5K races. There were no running shoes for women then, so she would wear nurse's shoes and run with him. After a few months, she could keep up with him, and they would run all over Boston together. But Bobbi wanted more. "I wanted to race in the Boston Marathon.

I didn't know if I even could run that distance. I just started to train. It wasn't a competitive thing, but more like love. You just fall for it. My boyfriend would drive me on his motorcycle to clock miles and then drop me off somewhere and see if I could run back to the house."

In the summer of 1964, while her parents were away in England on a sabbatical, Bobbi decided to put her malamute puppy in her Volkswagen bus and drive across the country to California, running all kinds of terrain along the way—a pretty radical act for her time. "I was young and had never seen the world before," she explains. "I wanted to see what the rest of the country was like." She set off alone and drove a couple of hundred miles to western Massachusetts, where she camped in the Berkshires and ran. Then she moved on. "I would just drive, find a logging road, park, take my sleeping gear out, hike up a mountain, and sleep in the wild."

In the mornings Bobbi would get up and run. In Kansas, she ran through the open plains. In Wyoming, she ran through grassy fields until she reached the Tetons. There were no running guides telling her how to train at that time, so she just figured every day she would run a little bit farther until she was running most of the day. "When I got out west, I was in awe. I had never seen anything like it. There was so much space. I got all the way to San Francisco and spent the night on the beach, then got up and ran. That was the first time I had seen the Pacific Ocean. I fell in love with it."

Bobbi was planning to run the Boston Marathon next spring, in April 1965. She trained hard all winter but sprained her ankle badly a month before the race and had to wait another year. In January 1966, she moved to Southern California to continue her training on the beaches around Del Mar. In February, she sent in her application for the Boston Marathon. Only then did she learn women could not participate.

"I got a letter back," she remembers, "and it said that women were not physiologically able to run twenty-six miles and, furthermore, that women were not allowed to compete, according to the international sporting regulation. The Athletic Amateur Union said that the longest run a woman was capable of was 800 meters. It never occurred to me that I wouldn't be able to run in Boston. This was all the more reason for me to run in the race—because they had something to learn. They thought the world was flat, so I was going to teach them it's round."

Still, Bobbi didn't know what would happen if she disregarded the regulations and did the race anyway. Would she get arrested and be thrown out? Would the men in the race bump her off the course because they were angry she was there? "When you do something outside the social norm, you don't know what to expect," says Bobbi. She would never know until she tried. "I took the bus back to Boston and arrived the day before the race. My parents were shocked because they didn't know I was coming. I knew they would have tried to dissuade me if I had told them ahead of time."

That day, even though the sun was shining brightly and it was hot, Bobbi had a blue hooded sweatshirt and a pair of her brother's shorts on. She pulled the hood up over her head and hid near the start in the bushes. When the gun went off, she jumped in the middle of the pack. After a while, she could hear the guys behind her trying to figure out whether or not she was a girl. She smiled and turned around to look at the guys behind her, and that was a defining moment. "If they had been angry, I wouldn't have been able to run. Instead, they exclaimed, 'You *are* a girl!' and started asking me all kinds of questions." Then the guys eventually convinced Bobbi to take off her hood. "It's a free road," said one man from Connecticut, Alton Chamberlin.

When Bobbi finally took her sweatshirt off, everyone—including those standing on the sidelines—could see she was a woman. And they started clapping for her. By the time she reached Wellesley, Bobbi's endeavor was being broadcast on the radio. The women came out of the school in droves to support her, crying, clapping, cheering. "I felt like I was setting people free," Bobbi says. "But I wasn't pushing. I was holding back, because I knew I had to finish. I was making a statement, and if I collapsed on the course, it would set women back."

A few miles outside of Boston, Bobbi's feet were bleeding from blisters and she was dehydrated. She didn't drink any water and had eaten a huge dinner the night before, thinking it would give her more energy. Suddenly, her pace dropped. She was heartbroken and afraid no one would be at the finish by the time she got there. But when she finally got to Dartmouth, the end of the race, everyone was still there. Alton and his friends were waiting for her, and he came over and put his arm around her. Even the governor of Massachusetts shook her hand. The next day, it was front-page news. "They couldn't believe a girl could run that. It was like I had flown to the moon."

□ □ □

Bobbi ran it again the next year, but she wasn't alone this time.

"Everyone thinks that crashing the Boston Marathon was the biggest thing I have ever done, but it was an accident," says Kathrine Switzer. "I didn't really think about the fact that women couldn't run that race." All of the guys on her track team at Syracuse University were going to run in the marathon, so she just wanted to run with them. She registered using her initials, K. T. Switzer. "I was reading J. D. Salinger at the time, so I thought I would just go by my initials, and no one would notice I was there," she explains.

Little did he know it, but her track coach—who, like others, didn't believe that Bobbi Gibb had actually run the whole marathon distance the year before—had egged her on. "I believed she *had* run it, and I wanted to show him that women *could* run a marathon," she says. "Besides, it felt heroic. Everyone said that I couldn't do it, and that women couldn't do it, and I knew I could. In those days, I didn't want to do it as a career. I just wanted to conquer the distance."

Kathrine started the race with her friends, but at mile 2, course marshal Jock Semple physically tried to pull her out of the race. (Bobbi Gibb was also running but had managed to slip by the officials.) As Semple approached Kathrine, teammate Thomas Miller blocked him, and Kathrine got away. Although she was officially disqualified, she finished in 4:20. Perhaps most importantly, an AP wire photographer witnessed and shot the whole confrontation, which is now widely known as "the Boston Incident," and the images were shown around the world the next day.

Kathrine remembers feeling confused as she continued to run that morning. She knew she couldn't quit, but she had mixed feelings of shame and anger. "I was inspired that day, but also angry and embarrassed. It was something that happened to me, not something I did." At the age of twenty, she was still treading the border between girlhood and womanhood. The girl in her had thought that running a marathon with her friends would be fun and was therefore shocked and embarrassed by the confrontation. The woman in her realized the implications of the incident and reacted with pride and anger. After her life-changing experience at the Boston Marathon, making changes in women's running became

Kathrine's life. She began writing newsletters, and she put together a seventy-five-page proposal to encourage more support for women's running. "My problem was that I felt really responsible after what happened with Jock Semple. I felt like I had this responsibility to show that I was right, and I devoted my life to it."

Her big break came in 1976, when she was hired by Avon to start the first-ever corporate-sponsored women's marathon. Two years later, the Avon Marathon, which drew in women from nine countries, was held in Atlanta, Georgia. A year later, in 1979, it drew in women from twenty-five countries, clearly disproving cynics who thought a women's marathon wouldn't be popular enough to be in the Olympics. From that it spawned a women's series of all kinds of runs, not just nationally, but internationally. It wasn't long before Avon was putting on four hundred international races of all kinds, involving over a million women from twenty-seven countries. Kathrine knows that it was the Avon races that led to women getting into the Olympics for distance running. And that is what she is most proud of in her life.

Today Kathrine can see the ramifications clearly. That one day in Boston set a course for her career as a writer, speaker, marathon commentator, and women's advocate. "Running a marathon was a sense of discovery," Kathrine says. "I came from an era of thousands of years of myths, where if a woman did anything stressful her uterus would fall out. I couldn't believe this. Every day I ran further and further. It was like being Columbus, and I was sailing a flat earth, so every day, I wondered when I would fall off. And then I didn't, and eventually I was lining up and pinning a number on."

□ □ □

"I started running because it was rebellious and nonconformist, and then it became a refuge during a tough period in my early twenties," says Jacqueline Hansen, who in 1973 won the Boston Marathon and in that same year became the first woman to break the 2:40 mark for a marathon for that distance in Eugene, Oregon. "Eventually it became my identity. But I stumbled onto marathons by accident."

Her first experience in marathons was from the sidelines, when Cheryl Bridges, one of her teammates from the (now disbanded) Los Angeles Track Club, decided to run a marathon in Culver City in 1971. "I went out to support her," Jacqueline says, "because I thought anyone crazy enough to run that distance was worth supporting."

The Los Angeles Track Club, like most athletic clubs of the time, consisted primarily of men, but it was progressive for its time. The coach was a Hungarian man named Lazlo Tabori. His workouts were tough—he had been trained by Igoli, another Hungarian, who is considered the founder of interval training. But most importantly, Lazlo didn't differentiate between men and women when it came to running. Jacqueline had no idea that her training was anomalous and admits that if she had known, she might have given up. "Our coach would group us according to speed, not gender, and that was a godsend," she says. "He didn't treat us women any differently from the guys, and that contributed to our success. When we first did the warm-up, I thought that was the workout! But staying with it and doing those hard workouts were what led me to holding world records. I was fortunate enough to benefit from it without having a clue about what I was doing."

Several of the first women record setters for distance hailed from the Los Angeles Track Club, such as Japanese-born Miki Gorman (who became a world-class marathon runner in her forties) and Jacqueline's friend Cheryl Bridges (the first woman to run a sub-2:50 marathon).

After Jacqueline saw Cheryl run a marathon in 1971, she realized she could do it too, and once she started doing them, it was a quick race to the top. She won the Boston Marathon in 1973 with a time of 3:05:59, and she set a world record at the Nike Oregon Track Club Marathon in 1975, running it in 2:38:19. With three international wins and a world record, she thought the obvious next step would be to aim for the Olympics.

That's when she realized there were no Olympic distance-running events for women. "I assumed that you would win your races and work up to Olympics, because that was true of shorter distances. So I won my first marathon, and I got serious about my training. I was naive enough to think that some petitions and lobbying would change the mind of the powers that be to let us in. But it became this long battle."

By 1977, Jacqueline became what she calls "an accidental feminist." She went to a National Organization for Women conference in Houston, Texas, and it was there that she realized how many bigger issues there were for women in the world—like simply the right to equal pay and jobs. In response, her first thought was, *So I can't run, what is the big deal?* But then, as the conference went on, she realized that the road to equal rights was paved by chain reactions, and any kind of breakthrough, whether big or small, would lead to more and bigger breakthroughs.

In 1983 Jacqueline heard a radio report from the American Civil Liberties Union discussing the fact that women had only a third of the Olympic events that men had. They wanted people to call in and talk about a potential lawsuit against the International Olympics Committee. "I couldn't call that number fast enough," says Jacqueline. In August 1984, the ACLU filed a suit on behalf of all women distance runners, seeking inclusion of the 5,000- and 10,000-meter races in the upcoming 1984 Olympics. The

ACLU didn't win in time for the 1984 Olympics, but the case created ongoing media attention that further raised awareness. The marathon ended up being included in the 1984 Olympics, but the 5,000- and 10,000-meter races were not put in until 1992.

"We used to make bad jokes about the dinosaurs on the International Olympics Committee. It was frustrating how many years it took, but I wouldn't change anything," says Jacqueline. "I feel proud to have been a part of getting women into the Olympics and into running marathons," says Jacqueline. "But I still try every chance I get to teach girls and women not to take anything for granted. I encourage women to give back to the sport in whatever way they can, and to remember their history, because there's a rarely told story there that fades with every new marathon."[1]

---

[1] For an inspirational look at early women runners, see Charlotte Lettis Richardson's documentary *Run Like a Girl*, which follows the lives of three women distance runners: Doris Brown Heritage, who ran in the '50s, '60s, and '70s; Charlotte herself, who ran in the turbulent '70s; and Camille Connelly, an eighteen-year-old contemporary distance runner.

Chapter Two: The Best Medicine

In February 2005, Diane Van Deren, a forty-five-year-old Colorado mom and professional runner, ran the Iditarod Trail Invitational in Alaska, where she covered 260 miles in below-freezing conditions,  hauling 42 pounds of gear on a sled before calling it quits. She hoped to cover 350 miles but fell short by 90 miles after tearing a groin muscle.

"I still managed to go about a hundred and eighty miles hauling my bad leg with my good leg," she remembers. "Then my good leg gave out." That was the end of that race—at least for then. She's hoping to do it again in 2007 and says that next time she'll complete her originally intended 350 miles.

But to Diane, the Iditarod was just one race. Over the next six months, she completed four back-to-back one-hundred-mile runs between June and September of 2005, including the prestigious Hardrock Hundred Mile Endurance Run, a 101.7-mile race in which runners climb a total of 33,000 feet through the San Juan Mountains around Silverton, Colorado.

Listening to Diane's list of races in 2005 is enough to make even a hardcore athlete tired. Yet she herself seems to have unlimited amounts of energy and drive, all of which she puts toward her family, her friends, and her cause: raising awareness about epilepsy.

□ □ □

Ten years ago, Diane suffered at least weekly from epileptic seizures, an experience that has given her tremendous motivation to succeed in extreme endurance runs and to promote greater awareness about an illness that is still not well understood. "Epilepsy is not a disease," she explains. "It's a neurological disorder that so few people really know anything about."

As she was growing up and becoming an adult, Diane had always felt easily disoriented, but she wrote it off to not resting enough or to training too hard. She would have these funny little feelings of déjà vu, her head would get light, and she would forget things and feel discombobulated. When she asked her husband, Scott, if he felt these things too, he said he didn't know what she meant. What she would later realize was that these early feelings were foreshadowing of what was to come with her epilepsy.

Diane and Scott were introduced by their mothers, who were in a church group together. They both loved sailing, biking, and hiking, and living in Colorado provided a perfect landscape for them to get outside often. They were married within a year of being introduced to each other and everything seemed perfect. They had two children right away and then were surprised with a third. That's when the seizures started. When Diane was twenty-four years old and pregnant with Matt, her third child, she had what she thought to be her first grand mal seizure. However, afterward, she found out from her mother that it wasn't her first. When she was sixteen months old, she came down with a high fever that lasted three days. Doctors did everything they could to control the fever, including packing her in ice, but at one point, it escalated to 105 degrees and led to a seizure that lasted for fifty minutes. Doctors weren't sure about the extent of the brain damage that might have resulted from the episode. But Diane recovered and grew up without any apparent problems. It often happens that children who suffer a seizure or even a few seizures "grow out of them" and never have one again. This seemed to be the case for Diane. But it wasn't.

About 2.7 million people in the United States live with varying degrees of epilepsy. Grand mal seizures are traumatic and draining: People usually collapse onto the ground, and the entire body tenses up like it is receiving shock treatment. They shake violently, can bite their tongues, and thrash about uncontrollably, which can result in injury. When the seizure is over, they are exhausted, and as Diane describes it, it's worse than running a hundred-mile race.

Life got scary in the Van Deren family after Diane's grand mal. Her three children grew up living in constant fear of the seizures because there was nothing they could do but clear the area, stand back, and watch when one came on. Being epileptic meant that Diane couldn't drive because she might crash the car. She couldn't take a bath alone because she might drown, and she couldn't go skiing because she might fall out of a chairlift. She rode horses and rode bikes but always left a note about where she was going because of the very real "what ifs."

Approximately 80 percent of epileptics are able to keep seizures at bay with the help of medication. In Diane's case, however, medication was not effective. Instead, she found her own unique form of treatment: running. Most epileptics experience what they call an "aura," a sense that a seizure is close at hand. When Diane would feel a seizure coming on, she would lace up her running shoes and head out the door. Running was the one activity that could somehow stave off the seizures. And while there is no scientific evidence showing that exercise can control seizures, Diane was positive that for her, running did.

However, she could only run so much in a day, and while the seizure might not come then or even for two days after a run, it would happen eventually. Sometimes they were minor seizures that simply left her disoriented, causing slurred speech, intense headaches, and a feeling of faintness. But other times, they would throw her to the ground, requiring her family to nurse her for up to a day afterward. "I tried everything to control my seizures. The only thing that controlled it was my running, so for me, that became my medicine."

Finally, in 1997, her doctor told her there was an experimental surgery that she might be a candidate for, a surgery that could possibly stop the seizures. Diane was immediately ready to try it, but her husband and doctor made her slow down and think twice about it because there was a chance the surgery could leave her totally incapacitated if her brain wasn't receptive. But she was willing to take the chance. "The seizures were more frustrating than the risk of death or of becoming a vegetable," Diane remembers. "They were controlling my life."

But before any surgery could be done, she had to first go through a series of tests to determine whether the epilepsy was located in the area of her brain that could be operated on. Diane was hooked up to electrodes and spent two days under a doctor's supervision, trying to bring on a grand mal seizure. This meant depriving herself of sleep, pedaling on a stationary bike, and running up and down the hallways of the hospital. Finally, after nearly two days, she felt one coming on, and she lay down and braced herself for it. The seizure was recorded on video, and Diane later watched it. Seeing herself having a seizure was incredibly emotional: For the first time, she knew what her family and friends had to deal with. "My poor kids must have been so scared all of those years," she says. "While I am having a seizure, I don't know what I look like. The body totally blocks it out. When the doctor showed that to me, that's when I understood."

In early 1997, Diane went into the hospital for brain surgery. The doctors would cut out the piece of her brain that was causing the seizures, a part of the right temporal lobe. It was risky, expensive surgery, but Diane and Scott felt like they had no other choice.

In the days following the surgery, Diane had a tube running out of the back of her head to drain fluids, and she was heavily medicated. At one point—perhaps because of the potent combination of a strong will and large doses of morphine—she pulled the tube out so she could escape and go running, a reaction she says was motivated by a primal fight-or-flight instinct.

"They hated me there," she says of the doctors and nurses who cared for her. "I was an awful patient. I must have looked like a crazy lady right after my surgery. I was running down the halls with my sleeping gown flapping open in the back and my butt exposed to the world," she says with a laugh. The part she doesn't laugh about is the fact that the doctors had to restrain her and strap her down to the bed so that she had no choice but to lie still. But she still couldn't be calmed down, so finally, the doctors were forced to put her into a drug-induced coma to allow her brain to heal peacefully.

The operation was a success, but that doesn't necessarily mean she will never have an episode again. Still, for now, it has allowed Diane to be seizure-free and off all medications for nine years. Unfortunately, as an effect of the surgery, her short-term memory was damaged. At times this frustrates her, but she's learned to cope by pasting little notes all over the house. Doctors' appointments, daughter Robin's basketball games, carpooling her son to work, upcoming races, interviews: These things all need notes.

However, forgetfulness can be a good thing. Diane likes that she forgets the trails she runs every morning. It makes running for hours on end always interesting, no matter how many times she has been on a trail. And when she's in a long-distance race, she is always able to balance the finish line with how she feels in the present. But in order to run so many miles successfully, she has to play some games with herself. "I always think the race starts at fifty miles," says Diane. "You have to pace yourself, eat right, drink lots of water. When I get to fifty, I want to feel good, and if I don't, it's going to be a really long day." She breaks the miles down in increments, counting ten miles at a time. She focuses on her footwork, her body's rhythm; she visualizes the challenges she has in front of her but always remembers to bring herself back to the present.

"I run in the moment," she says, "especially so with my brain injury. It's a little overwhelming for me to think about the distance. It would be for anyone. I don't get ahead of myself too much. I just think about my footwork, my body, my rhythm. I don't think about what's going to happen at mile seventy. I just feel like whatever happens, happens, and I will deal with it."

Reporters who have interviewed Diane always want to know how she reminds herself to eat and drink and where she's stashed her stuff if she's so forgetful. One of the keys to a major race is strategically planting food and water all along the hundred miles or so of a racecourse. This takes careful planning ahead of time and then of course, remembering to eat and drink when you get to that spot. With her spotty memory, one would think this would be a problem. "It's funny, but running distance races is actually relaxing in many ways. I don't have to worry about whether I forgot something that my daughter told me or to pick up my son from somewhere. All I have to do is run and think about what comes next."

That's why when Diane was first invited to run the Iditarod, she thought it sounded like an amazing challenge, as well as a great way to raise money for the Children's Hospital in Denver. The day the run began, it was thirty degrees below zero. The runners left ten days before the mushers with their dogs. Her goal was to cover 350 miles over a week.

"I had no idea about the elements or how I would feel out there. You have to be totally self-sufficient. There's no support." Before departing, she had to sign a waiver releasing the race-holders from any accountability should she be attacked by a bear or moose. As it turned out it wasn't a moose attack but a moose hole on a dark night that caused her harm.

"I was looking for the reflectors that they have out there to show the mushers where they are going, and I stepped into the hole. My leg went all the way in it up to my thigh, and because I was on a hill, my sled pulled me back, and I tore my groin muscle."

In spite of the injury, she ran another 180 miles. "Every mile I ran made another dollar for the Children's Hospital. All of these sponsors were counting on me." Finally, at mile 260, with a hugely swollen ankle and suffering from hallucinations from the pain and exhaustion, she could push no further.

"I was extremely frustrated that I couldn't finish. I felt great but my ankle was so huge I couldn't get it in the shoe. There was just no getting around that, so I had to give it up," she says of the experience.

Throughout her running career, Diane has never worried over whether she could finish a race—but she has worried about not being allowed to race at all. "When I first started racing ultras, I never revealed my previous medical history," she says. "But now, pretty much everyone racing around me knows, so I've decided, 'Oh well, if a race organizer doesn't want me in, too bad.' I think it's important that people see me doing this and know that I had epilepsy."

But all that is less relevant these days, as Diane's impressive results have firmly cemented her in the ultra trail-running scene. In June 2005, she received the prestigious Everest Award for Female Trail Runner of the Year—a sort of Oscar for exceptional athletes in disciplines such as trail running and kayaking.

"I dedicated this award to a little friend who passed away several days prior to the ceremony," Diane says. "Hunter Nelson was only five years old and died of a seizure in his sleep. With his passing, I feel my role in sports needs to be utilized to help others who are still working through medical struggles like epilepsy."

"We all have trials in life," she continues. "Everybody has trials, but people see me performing, and I feel like it helps them. I am a runner, a musician, a mother, a speaker. What people don't know until I tell them is that I struggle daily with a brain injury."

Diane swears that running a hundred miles is "therapy" for her brain. "It's just downtime, when I am not stimulated," she explains. Still, Diane admits, sometimes her memory loss and single-minded passion for running can be nerve-wracking for her family. Once, she packed up the car and headed out to a race in Montana, a state away, but forgot to tell the kids she was going to be gone for the race. In the early evening, when she didn't come home, they started to worry because their dad was out of town on a business trip. When she called around 8:00 PM, they had just been debating about whether to call the police, worried that she had a seizure while out running (her shoes were gone).

"I can be pretty focused at times," she admits with a laugh. "Multitasking can be very difficult. So I concentrate on one thing at a time to do things well. Especially when I am packing for a hundred-mile race, or like when I ran the Iditarod. I needed to be very focused on what I brought. Forgetting one item, such as an extra headlamp or batteries or a jacket, could have life-threatening consequences."

□ □ □

In 1996, right before her surgery, Diane had the opportunity to go to Washington, D.C., to champion her cause. The Epilepsy Foundation of America sent her to represent others with epilepsy and to lobby for new seizure medications. At the time, she remembers lawmakers talking about not having enough research.

"I was like, *Hello,* I am a real live rat on a wheel! You need volunteers, here I am! I am living it and dealing with it!' I do feel like I made a difference, putting a real-life story in front of Congress."

What she told Congress is similar to what she says when she gives motivational talks: There need to be solutions for epilepsy, and more research. She likes to say that running saved her from defeat when she had epilepsy. Now, especially in the more grueling races, it helps remind her that she's alive.

Despite her struggles, Diane has no complaints. "I wouldn't change anything that has happened in my life," she says. "But it hasn't been easy, and I have no guarantees that the seizures won't start again. That's why I get up early. Because now I like to get in a full day and soak in all the life that I can."

Chapter Three: Marathon Mom

When Kristin Armstrong married cyclist Lance Armstrong in 1998, she never could have predicted how different her life would be five years later. After a whirlwind courtship and marriage, three children, and her husband's rise to fame, Kristin and Lance divorced in 2003. It was during this challenging time that she discovered her inner athlete.

You would think that if a woman was ever to discover her inner athlete, it would be when she was married to one of the most famous athletes in the world. But it wasn't so simple. "I had never had an interest in being competitive with athletics, because being married to Lance was very consuming, and I got to live the competitiveness through him," Kristin explains.

Growing up, she had never really been involved in sports, mostly because of her family situation. Kristin's dad was an executive for IBM, and so they were always moving. As a result, she didn't join any organized sports teams or clubs. "As a kid, it was hard to get involved with anything because we moved every two years," Kristin remembers. "I was more of an academic child than an athletic child. I got into jogging a little bit in my twenties, so when I met Lance, I was running twenty minutes here and there. Then, once we were settled in Austin, I wanted to build a life."

In the aftermath of her divorce, two of her best friends in Austin—Kristen Turner, or KT, and Paige Alam, both runners—thought that running might be a good tonic for Kristin and convinced her to join them on a morning run.

"I never wanted to know how far we were going," Kristin recalls of those early training runs. "I didn't wear a watch or keep track. I just showed up with my running clothes on and let them lead me around."

Within a few weeks, Kristin's friends were able to take her on a long run—ten miles. She was in a haze back then, because she wasn't sleeping or eating well. "I am sure I was lethargic and sad, but being in their company was the lift I needed," she remembers.

Thus began Kristin's life as a runner. Every Saturday morning from that day on, Paige, KT, and Kristin—and sometimes a handful of other women—have run distances spanning five to twenty-two miles. The group is casual, not really an organized club, more a gathering of friends. On Wednesdays, they have a coach, Cassandra Henkiel, so they jokingly call themselves "Cassie's Quick Chicks." Many of the women are moms, and many are training for marathons, triathlons, or whatever race might be coming their way.

Running gave Kristin quality time with her friends—time when she didn't have to chase children around or answer endless phone calls from the press about her divorce. And for the first time in years, she had a few hours a week that were for herself. At the same time as she grew physically stronger from the runs, she could feel herself growing emotionally stronger.

"When I started running, I felt really empty," she says. "I was tired and distracted. I was tired of making decisions. I would just show up, and we would run, and that was that. I couldn't take on anything else at that time."

KT and Paige were immediately impressed with Kristin's natural running ability and stick-to-it attitude. The next step, they thought, was a marathon. When they told her she was ready to do the Dallas White Rock Marathon in December 2003, a mere three months after she started running, she laughed at them. Sure, she had run twenty miles with them a few times. *But a marathon?* she first thought. *No way.*

But the marathon would give her a goal. After considering it more, she decided, why not? "I felt like, if I can get through one monumental thing like a divorce, it will transfer into other areas of my life. It's confidence-building, knowing you can go that deeply into sadness and pain, and then be okay. The marathon helped show me that there would be an end to my sadness, just like there is an end to a marathon. It hurt while I was doing it, and it hurt afterward, but then it's like, *Okay, what's next?*"

After the marathon, which she ran in 3:47, Kristin thought she was done with marathons, although she continued running with her group of women friends. She says that running had become almost as important as her morning prayers; it helped her find calm and strength within herself. Soon after she finished the marathon, she wrote a letter to her running group, thanking them for their support and the inspiration. Many of her thoughts and sentences were very powerful: "I am not an athlete. I have washed clothes for an athlete, massaged an athlete, bandaged wounds for an athlete, cheered my heart out for an athlete, prepared pasta al dente for an athlete, but never in my thirty-two years did I consider any athletic potential living within the confines of my own body."

Her friends were so moved and impressed with her words that they encouraged her to send it to *Runner's World*—and she did. The letter, titled "The Next Big Step" (August 2004), touched readers—especially women runners—so deeply that Kristin was hired as a regular writer and given a contributing editor title. Since that first column in September 2004, she has written about running with her kids, about learning to appreciate the mud and grit of a good trail run, and about her running-obsessed hometown of Austin, Texas. But mostly she has written about finding and nurturing her own inner runner.

When she and Lance first met, Kristin was working for a public relations firm and had especially enjoyed the writing part of her job. Writing was in Kristin's blood, but prior to her marriage, she didn't realize how much it meant to her. After becoming a columnist, she grew more confident, and another idea formed: She decided to write a devotional for women who are going through divorce. Scheduled for publication in January 2007, the book is titled *Happily Ever After: Finding Peace and Courage Through a Year of Divorce.*

"I just wished I had something to turn to like that when I was in the thick of things," she says. "Writing has been therapeutic. It's been a way to take something that wasn't a good experience and make something nice about it."

Katie McDonald Neitz is the senior editor at *Runner's World* and edits Kristin's monthly column. While the column wasn't edited by Katie in the beginning, she was excited to later be assigned to it, as she had been following Kristin's writing since she started contributing to the magazine. "I will admit at first I wondered, *Why is Lance Armstrong's ex-wife writing for us?* I think people often have a one-sided view of these things when we hear about someone so public."

But Katie's opinion on the matter turned around right away. "Her pieces speak to our audience. They talk about a mother wanting to quit running a marathon but knowing she can't because she doesn't want her kids to think it's okay to quit. She talks about learning new things about herself, her town, her family—through running. She shows herself as a regular person, and she's very honest. In one of her early columns, she mentioned Lance and her divorce, and how it was hard to get out of bed. Most of us deal with events in our life privately—things like divorce and learning how to run—but she has dealt with it all publicly. My heart went out to her when I started reading her column, and I didn't even know her."

Kristin says she finds writing to be a release much like running. Every once in a while, she'll write a sentence that will feel so right, it makes her want to cry. "That keeps me going through the motions as long as it takes, just to get another taste of that. Just like the runners high, elusive and profound—and addictive!" she says. "I think people like me because my perspective is that of a mom who enjoys running. I am not someone who has big things to tell you about my split times."

But that's not to say she doesn't train. Currently, she runs five days a week, three to five miles per day. When she's training for a marathon, she ups her mileage on the weekends. And when she travels, she takes her shoes, even if she's just going overnight. "I like how you see a city in a different light when you are on your feet instead of in a car. You can feel more of its spirit and understand the community better if you go for a run in a new place," she says.

In May 2005, Kristin tried something totally new—trail running. When Scott Dunlap—the husband of a close friend and a competitive trail runner who can brag a personal record of 1:14 in a half marathon—invited her to join him on a rugged and challenging run through Woodside, California, she was game.

"In the month leading up to my visit, Scott tested my Girly Meter with emails about losing a toenail, his eternal case of poison oak, and odd places to find ticks," she wrote in her column. "He once sent a post-race photo of a dude with gory red streaks down the front of his shirt, with the subject line of 'Nipple Chafing.' To which I replied: 'Nursed twins. Next?'"

When Kristin got to Northern California, it was a rainy, cold day. The thermometer read forty-eight degrees. For a gal from Texas, she might as well have been in Vail, Colorado, midwinter without a coat. The plan was two runs—a short one in Huddart Park followed the next day by a ten-miler through a redwood area called Purisima Creek. She was a trooper, showing up at breakfast for the runs in rain gear—and of course a white shirt, waterproof mascara, and lip gloss. Scott took one look at her that first day and wondered if he had made a big mistake.

"When she showed up, I thought, *Oh boy, she's going to hate this.* But her tiptoes around the mud quickly turned into charging right through at full throttle."

By mile 6, Scott said Kristin was leading the way up the steepest terrain he could find, and she wanted more. "She's a very strong runner when she taps into her determination. When it happens, it's amazing how quickly she can turn fear into fun."

Kristin wrote about this first trail running experience a few months later in a much more modest way.

We started running, and I felt my inexperience as I tried to keep up. My breathing was uneven, and I fumbled for my stride. I took in my surroundings in choppy, blurry, Blair Witch visuals.

"Don't follow my footsteps," Scott said. "You have to pick a path for yourself. What works for me probably isn't best for you." He let me take the lead, and my confidence grew. . . . We got back in the pickup and sat in silence for a moment until Scott said, "You weren't as much of a chick as I thought." I flipped down the visor mirror and checked my bad self out.

I pointed out that my waterproof mascara and long-lasting pink lip gloss had held up remarkably well. He sighed, and we headed home.
—Runner's World, *Kristin Armstrong, July 2005*

About Kristin's writing, Scott says, "She has had the gift of writing her whole life. My wife has shown me notes that Kristin passed her as a kid, and they are eloquent, honest, and absolutely hilarious. It's not a surprise that she writes for a major magazine— just that it took her this long to do it. I am glad she has allowed herself to share her experiences with the world, even after so much time in the unforgiving public eye. We're all the better for it."

Although Kristin has been writing her column for a year and a half, she is still surprised that she has become well-known through her running and writing, particularly among women. But she is glad that she has the column to share her feelings about running, motherhood, and life. "I think the reason I strike a chord with some women is because they can relate to me—I'm an average athlete, I'm a single mom, I'm trying to do many things well at once," she says. "Raising my kids, growing my career, staying fit and healthy, staying faith-filled, all of it. They know it's awesome, and exhausting."

Discovering her inner runner has been an exciting journey, one that Kristin hopes will continue to inspire other women. But she says it's not the running alone that has kept her strong—her Christian faith has also been a key element. She and Paige Alam often send silent prayers to those in need during their training and races.

While Kristin may see herself as an average runner, her best marathon time of 3:35—from the October 2005 Chicago Marathon—puts her in the upper range of her age group. "I can't fathom that I am really that fast. I certainly don't feel fast. What does fast feel like?" Kristin asks. "I guess I felt fast that day when I ran 3:35. But more than anything, I felt healthy, happy, free, and ready to go. I still thank God for that day."

Kristin remembers it perfectly. The weather was sunny and warm, and while she felt a little nervous, she was also excited about the race. She ate a peanut butter and jelly sandwich with coffee. She drank a bunch of water and Gatorade and then headed to the start line. She had spent the day before visualizing, and she had a supply of fig bars in her pocket, and an Icy Hot cream ready to slap on should she start getting leg cramps. But she told herself she wouldn't get leg cramps. She had been training, and she was ready. She and Paige lined up at the start line and then were off.

During the marathon, the two devoted every mile to a different person in their lives who needed prayers. They came up with the idea a few weeks before the race and wrote down lists of people they wanted to pray for. "We were surprised at how similar our lists were when we compared," says Kristin. For her, the most powerful prayers came at the end of her marathon, when she thought about Paige's daughter, Layne, who wears a brace on her left leg. "You can become so body centric when you're running distances. With our prayers, it wasn't about us and how we felt. It was about other people, and even if you are suffering in that moment, you are just thinking about that."

For Kristin, who is notorious for getting cramps in her calves after mile 20, Layne provided her much-needed relief that day. "Layne was mile 25 for me. I was slapping Icy Hot all over my leg, and I just kept going. I thought about how much courage it takes her every day to get on and off the bus and carry her backpack. I thought, *I don't care what happens to my calf, she has to deal with that every day*. Instead of thinking about me, I was thinking about Layne and praying for her. It felt like a more active prayer to have the pain. It was more of a sacrifice."

The Chicago Marathon was a turning point for Kristin. Paige remembers, "It was symbolic for her, and everyone could see it. There was not all of this residual pain. The baggage she had was just left behind as she ran. So much ground has been covered, literally and figuratively speaking. She's healthy and happy now."

It's not just Kristin's monthly column, but her day-to-day attitude and choices that inspire those around her. "What I learned from her experience," Paige says, "and what I think other women see, is that you make a choice somewhere down the line. All women do. You ask yourself, 'What will I do with this pain?' and the choice Kristin has made is one that so many women struggle with. What she does is she runs, she writes, she cares for her kids, and continues on. Seeing her gives others hope that everything does turn around."

Chapter Four: Rusching Around the World

There are three things Rebecca Rusch will never forget about racing in Vietnam in May 2002: the leeches, the intense heat, and the feeling that her father was traveling alongside her. It was day four and

another scorching hot day in Vietnam for the Raid Gauloises, a multiday adventure race. By that point, Rebecca and her four male teammates had lost count of how many leech-infested rice paddies they had run through and how many jungle mountain passes they had climbed over. At times, their skin was so prickly from the intense heat that at night, they traveled over the dark trails completely naked, holding their packs in front of them to avoid the chafing of their sweat-soaked clothing and backpack straps.

Vietnam was emotional for Rebecca, not because of the physical discomfort of the jungle or the normal intensity of racing but because this was where she lost her father. During the Vietnam War, he had been a fighter pilot and was shot down over Laos in 1972. She was only four at the time and barely remembered him. More than thirty years later, here in the Vietnamese jungle, she felt both his presence and her own power to conquer any obstacle in her path.

She also felt humbled: As she made her way through the thick jungle foliage, she looked up to see an elderly Vietnamese couple heading up a steep dirt footpath nearby. "I remember thinking, *How bumbling and out of place we must look to these people!* There they were, almost walking up this mountainside, virtually sweat-free, looking as if it's a stroll in the park, and we were dripping and exhausted."

By the time the couple reached them, Rebecca's team was half hiking, half stumbling up the path that led from a rice paddy into the jungle. It was the sixth day of the race, with one day to go. This was the last hiking section—after that, there would be twenty hours of paddling, but at least they would be off their aching feet. For now, the top of the mountain was still two hours in front of them.

Rebecca remembers the Vietnamese woman looking directly into her eyes, and she knew the woman could sense how exhausted she was. The woman reached out, put her hand on the small of Rebecca's back, and urged her forward, up the hill, for a few minutes. Then the couple went on past Rebecca and her teammates.

A bit farther up the mountain, Rebecca saw the couple again. They were obviously concerned about her and her teammates and were waiting for them under the shade of a tree. They joined the team again, staying on until they were all up and over the mountain—an elevation gain of a few thousand feet.

"I am always in awe when I go to these places. We are supposed to be some of the best athletes in the world, yet when we are out of our element, we can be reduced to nothing," she recalls.

□ □ □

Adventure racing is a relatively unknown sport and usually requires a bit of explaining, at least to Americans. The sport finally got some recognition in the mid-'90s when TV producer Mark Burnett of *Survivor* fame brought the Eco-Challenge to television viewers across America. Prior to that, it was mainly an obscure style of racing that only the French, British, New Zealanders, and Australians partook in.

Depending on the race location, an adventure racing team will run, bike, hike, kayak, ski, in-line skate, climb, or even ride camels or horses—all while navigating their way through jungles or mountain ranges sometimes as far away as Borneo or Tibet. Often, they've never been to the place they are traveling through, so every bend in the road and every section they bushwhack is a mystery—which means they need to be physically prepared for anything.

Not many people can become a professional adventure racer. It takes tenacity, natural athletic talent, and the ability to control the mind when the body is screaming at you to quit. Very few have the mettle to be proficient in a multitude of sports and to do them for days on end without physically crashing. Because of the travel, it's also an expensive sport, and it requires a lot of gear. Adventure racers have to be more than just strong runners, cyclists, and rock climbers—they have to be able to do everything for hours on end.

Rebecca has had top-five finishes in nearly every international race she's completed—impressive, considering only 50 percent of the teams ever finish. Where did she get the drive and commitment that are so indispensable for adventure racing? Rebecca credits her mother, Judy, who spent Rebecca's childhood a widow, trying to work her way up the corporate ladder in order to support her two daughters. "I really look up to my mom because it couldn't have been easy to go on with life after my father's death. She became a computer programmer during a time when women weren't doing that. She eventually became a top executive in a man's world. It's funny—now I am in a man's world too, and I too have excelled in it. For some reason, I like that challenge, just as my mom did."

As a young girl, Rebecca spent a lot of time playing outside but didn't get started as a runner until high school. "I was a good runner, so I did well on a very talented team of girls who believed in me before I believed in myself. It was the first thing I ever did that was organized, and so it definitely formed who I am as a person. I am not sure what I would be doing if I hadn't joined the team. It definitely shaped me into a team player, into a competitor, into a hard worker, and into someone who knows what it's like to win and lose gracefully."

She joined the varsity squad when she was a freshman, which she admits was a bit intimidating, especially considering she had originally only joined the track team because her neighbor told her she would get a free tracksuit and that it would help her control her weight. She was a scrawny tomboy, but like most teen girls, she suddenly feared fat.

But track turned out to be more than a cool suit and a slim body. She eventually became the varsity team captain and led her team to state in cross-country. Her races were the 800, 1,600, 3,200 meter, and 2-mile relay. While running the 800 was satisfying, cross-country was her passion. "What I loved about cross-country was being in the grass and that every course is different. I liked being in the trees and jumping over logs, and that sort of wilderness aspect—as much as you could get in the Chicago suburbs. That's what appealed to me."

Rebecca continued track and cross-country in college, but she didn't find the same joy in it. She felt like the women on the team were competing against each other instead of with each other and that the coach wasn't supportive. He made the team turn in logs of what they'd eaten over the weekend, and then he would take out a highlighter and start slashing through the bad things they ate, announcing them loudly, for everyone to hear. "For me, it just created all of these issues with food and feelings that I wasn't good enough. It was just totally opposite of high school, where I was told that I was good, where it was more of a supportive atmosphere," Rebecca recalls.

When she was twenty-five, she moved from the Midwest to California. This is when she returned to running, and when she became interested in paddling as well. She joined an outrigger canoe team, and they would train by running up and down the beaches around Los Angeles.

It was in 1998 that Rebecca first heard about the newly emerging multidiscipline sport of adventure racing. She learned of it from a few of the top competitors, who came to Rockreation, the rock-climbing gym she worked at in Los Angeles, to learn how to rappel down a cliff for an upcoming race they had in Utah. This seemed odd to Rebecca, as climbers usually think of rappelling as something you do after you reach the top. The racers invited Rebecca to come to an adventure racing camp in Malibu a few weeks later.

"The last night of the camp, we had a trail run in the middle of the night that was optional. Most of the guys on my team were like, 'No way am I getting up.' I figured we were just there for the weekend so I should go for it." She did, and this impressed the camp leaders so much that a few weeks later, she got a call from one of the coaches, who asked her to be on their team for an upcoming race.

She had hardly mountain biked and was just figuring out the whole trail running thing, but knew she was a strong paddler, so she figured, why not? "I entered this race because I was bored. It was winter; I was working a lot and wanted something to kick-start my motivation. I was invited to do this crazy twenty-four-hour race, and without really knowing what it was, I said yes so that I'd have a goal out there to push me in my daily workouts." Her team won the race.

As Rebecca stood on the podium and people from some of the top adventure-racing teams came up to her to congratulate her and find out whether she was excited about going to Australia, all she could think was, *What have I just gotten myself into?* The race she'd just finished turned out to have been the qualifier for the 1998 Eco-Challenge in the Australian Outback. Their win secured her team free entry into the international race, which would take place two months later.

The Eco-Challenge was her first international race. While her team started off strong, one of her teammates burned out before they made it through forty-eight hours, and the team dropped out. She was disappointed as she watched the race continue on without them. As she thought back on it, she knew her mistake in that race was that she should have spoken up. After her years of training for track, it was obvious to her that they were going too hard. But as she was the novice and the only female on the team, she wasn't comfortable voicing her thoughts.

"On the first night, when we were running through the desert at the very front of the seventy-team pack, this other racer, one of the top U.S. racers at the time and one of my instructors from the camp, Cathy Sassin, came up behind me, put her hand on my arm, and said, 'Be careful.' She knew we would burn out. She had the experience, and she was giving me warning in a kind way instead of telling me what would happen. Sure enough, she was right."

As the rest of the teams continued on, Rebecca watched the race longingly, wishing she had been more vocal with her team. But she learned a lot. She learned that she had to speak up for herself, regardless of what the guys thought. And she learned her body was capable of a lot more than she had ever imagined. What she thought was going to be a one-time thing ended up becoming her career. That first big race lit a fire in her. She was not a quitter, and so the Australia competition left her with a strong desire to finish one of these unbelievably long races. She's been adventure racing ever since.

□ □ □

Like anyone, Rebecca has sometimes experienced doubt—but she has found ways of turning that doubt into drive. "The starting line for adventure racing is always the worst, because it seems like every race starts with running. The men all feel the need to go hard out of the start line, so that first day is hell. I am holding on for dear life and having this internal monologue the whole time. *Am I good enough for this? Did I train enough? Am I going to make it? Are they going to slow down?* It's always the same at the start of every race, and then, by the second day, they mellow out. I find my groove, and my confidence inevitably returns."

She adds, "In adventure racing, you're not choosing your own pace, really, you're choosing the pace of the team, and so that's all rolled into the challenge as well. This can be especially intense when you are a woman. While all teams are required to have a woman on the team, there is that underlying intimidation, that feeling of not wanting to be the slowest one. That's always in my head. So this is why I run. It keeps me ahead of the pack. It makes me think, *I can do this.*"

In Rebecca's opinion, running is the one sport that's a true test of your athletics, because there's nothing mechanical to depend on. "Running is pure," she says. "You have to depend on your body to get you there, so there's nothing to hassle with. No tires to pump up or special shorts to find. You just put on your shoes and go."

She uses running as her base training for everything, whether it be a twenty-four-hour mountain bike race in Moab or a six-day adventure race through Patagonia. "There's something that running does for your body. It just gets you really fit really fast. It just gets you strong. I don't know why. Maybe it's because all the bones and everything—you're supporting your own weight, whereas on a bike or paddling you're sitting on another piece of machinery that's supporting a piece of you. In running, there's no copout. Your legs have to push you forward; your own weight has to be moved by you."

Since becoming a full-time adventure racer, Rebecca has competed in over forty international multiday races—including the most difficult race in the world, the Raid Gauloises (four times), and the high-profile Eco-Challenge (eight times). The team that Rebecca captained for four years, Team Montrail, won the Raid Gauloises in Kyrgyzstan in 2002.

Beyond a strong roster of wins, Rebecca has been recognized in other ways. In 2003, she was named Adventure Racer of the Year by *Competitor* magazine. She has also formed a number of women-only teams, putting aside her better chances of winning in order to show the world that women can compete in what has so far been primarily a sport for men. In 2000, she raced in Patagonia with a team that consisted of one man and three women; they placed fourth.

"She's super-strong and consistent," says Danelle Ballengee, who raced on a two-person team with Rebecca in a 2005 women-only adventure race in Spain. Danelle has also raced against Rebecca numerous times over the last few years on their coed teams. "She is good at all the disciplines, but she's definitely a strong runner. She's better at off-trail running and orienteering and bush-bashing stuff. She has a good sense of direction and is good at getting over things." When Danelle says this, she means Rebecca is literally good at getting over things. The rockier the path in front of her, the faster Rebecca moves.

Anna Keeling, of Team Golite/Timberland, who has also raced with and against Rebecca over the years, says she's an athlete whom many women look up to because they can relate to her. "She is very real and has normal hang-ups with her sport, but she never gives up. She's quite a fighter."

In 2000, at the Raid Gauloises in Tibet, Rebecca had one of the toughest run/hikes of her life. After 3,000 feet of elevation gain on mountain bikes, the racers switched as quickly as possible to hiking gear. For those who have never been at 14,000 feet, it's a long way from what we recognize as "the ground." At this altitude, every step is as slow as walking through thick mud, so there were times when all the competitors could do was walk—if that.

This portion of the race proved to be one of the most challenging of Rebecca's career. As the team pushed on up the steep mountainside, Rebecca's running slowed to a walk, and then, all she could do was crawl. She felt like she was suffocating. "I am not sure when I became aware of the feeling, but I knew I was in trouble," she says now. As the sky darkened to black, her team ascended slowly with a mule they named Bessie. Bessie was weighted down with gear because another teammate was also struggling.

Rebecca kept quiet because she was sure her discomfort would go away once they descended. But as they neared the summit, she found herself gasping for tiny bits of oxygen. "My lungs felt as if I could only suck in about a quarter capacity. My legs were wobbling underneath me, and I was dizzy. This was the highest I'd been before." She was aware of the symptoms of altitude sickness, but she knew it wasn't the altitude. It was something else. "The fact that I might be having a heart attack weighed heavily in my mind."

As it turned out, Rebecca had gotten an asthma attack from the incredible amount of dust at the unusually high start line (14,000 feet). As they ascended to 17,500 feet, her lungs, filled with dust particles, were damaged permanently. She now suffers from asthma regularly—which she didn't before this race. As a professional athlete, this has become Rebecca's ongoing challenge.

"Once I was diagnosed, it was like, *Ahhhh—that's better.* I'm fighting an uphill battle, but at the same time, once I knew, it was refreshing to know it wasn't just me not getting into shape. There was a medical reason for why I wasn't breathing very well," says Rebecca. "I still struggle with it and have to take care of it. I have to warm up really well—especially in big changes in cold air or humid air. All those things affect me, especially when I am running."

But in that moment at 17,500 feet in Tibet, Rebecca, for the first time in her life, felt like her sport was seriously jeopardizing her life. Flashing back to her early days of discovering adventure racing, she realized that she did not sign up for these sports to hurt or kill herself. She loved the challenge, she loved the travel to exotic places, she loved running through the mountains at a fast pace—but damaging her body had never been a motive. She remembers sitting near the top of the empty mountain. "All I could think about was, *What if I died here today? Am I ready to die?* There was no one to help me there. No helicopter could rescue me; my teammates could not help me any more than they already were. They were already carrying my pack and towing me on a rope."

As Rebecca stood there, hunched over her trekking poles, she realized the only way to escape the fear and torture were to continue forward with the team and descend to lower ground. "That was one of the only times I remember my mind giving in and the fear eating away at my confidence. The moment you take the time to let the insecure voices in your head be heard and let your own fear come to the forefront of your mind, your race is over," explains Rebecca.

It was camaraderie that kept her going. "All I needed was someone to acknowledge my fear and to tell me it was okay to stop if I had to—and one of my teammates did that. He knew what I needed up there to keep going. Just knowing I had someone supporting me mentally gave me the strength I couldn't generate on my own. That's where I think it's important to have a team if you are really going to push yourself."

In Tibet, there was a moment when she almost quit, but eventually, she found enough strength to cover the four seemingly impossible kilometers that moved them toward lower elevation, where her breathing got easier. She made it to a medical tent and got antibiotics, and her team finished seventh. It was the highest all-American finish ever, and it is still one of the career achievements she's most proud of.

□ □ □

Rebecca attributes some her passion for adventure racing to her national identity. "Americans have an obsession with the extreme. Marathons are commonplace now; the Ironman is no big deal. People are pushing further and further. Everyone is trying to figure out how they can be the first to do something. Someone said to me recently that the whole world has already been mapped and discovered. Adventure racers have the same mindset as early explorers, but they can't find new territory in terms of land," says Rebecca. "So we're exploring inside ourselves. We're exploring the limits of the human body and mind. I really like to think of it in that way. Every race holds a new lesson for me, a new territory to explore. It never gets old, and it's never the same."

She admits she might also be addicted to the excitement of the races, and to the peace she experiences as a result of them. "It dulls everyday life—in a good way, though," she says. "It makes me not stress about the little stuff. My credit card company called and reminded me I hadn't made a payment in forever. In the past, I would have probably been freaking out about that stuff. But I'm not. It's not important. However, I do wonder if I'll always need these super-intense experiences to feel happy. If it's been too long, I need it. I crave it. I made a pact with myself to do something major on every birthday, so at the very least, I'll do that. I need to remind myself of who I am."

As an adventure racer, Rebecca is constantly redefining the edges of her comfort zone. One of her favorite quotes is "Pain is weakness leaving the body." This mantra, as well her sense of camaraderie, comes to her aid when she's struggling.

"I usually don't stop during a race because it takes all I can muster just to keep up with my team," she says. "Often, there isn't even time for me to go to the bathroom or fill my water bottle. There are tons of times every race when I am miserable and I am running behind a teammate who is towing me. There are so many times when I look at my teammates—if I can see them through my blurred vision—and feel like they're family. There are also times when I am excited, panicked, weary, hateful, wishing I could stop— you name the emotion. Then I look around and realize I feel so lucky to be in such an incredible place—until the guys tell me to hurry up," she adds with a smile.

Rebecca believes people have to find their joy in fitness and to find inspiration in whatever they put their energy into. "I have made choices in my life to create situations that make me feel alive and excited. Of course, I sometimes plod away, bored on a treadmill just to put the miles in. However, in the back of my mind, I know I am doing that work in preparation for an upcoming event that I'm really excited about, and that makes it all worth it. Anyone can plod away on a treadmill for thirty minutes, three days a week, for fitness. But not everyone has the guts or reaps the benefits of going out on the weekend and running in the hills, or signing up for a ten-K race. Getting out of your comfort zone and finding out who you are is really what running is about."

Chapter Five: The Transformation of a Runner

For any female runner in her late fifties, running a sub-seven-minute mile is an amazing accomplishment. But this running time disappoints Janet Furman Bowman. There was a time in the not-so-distant past when Janet—a longtime runner and former president of Marin County's Tamalpa Runners—was one of the fastest in the group. But that was in the '80s and '90s, and this is now—now that she's a woman, that is.

As a male-to-female transsexual, losing her running speed is one of the hardest things Janet has had to adjust to.

At the age of fifty, Janet (she now eschews her former male name) was a single, affluent, healthy man who was close to retiring after twenty-five years as CEO of a successful electronics company. After graduating from Columbia in 1969 with a degree in electrical engineering, Janet began a career in the flourishing San Francisco rock music scene. In the early '70s, she toured with the Grateful Dead and other bands, specializing in live recordings. In 1974, she founded Furman Sound, a pioneering manufacturer of professional audio equipment. Over the years, her company prospered. By 1999, when she sold the controlling interest and retired from day-to-day operations, the company had seventy-five employees and over a hundred products.

These days, life is much simpler. She still lives the comfortable life of a relatively young retiree, sharing a spacious home with her life partner, Laurie, and Laurie's twelve-year-old daughter. But it wasn't long ago when her life seemed a lot more confusing. Ever since she was a child, she knew she wasn't meant to be male.

"I had fantasies about being female dating from about age five. As a preteen, I used to read my older sister's *Seventeen* magazine in secret. I observed girls and women with utter fascination, but from a distance. Later on, I experimented with wearing my sister's clothes, but I didn't know why I felt compelled to do this. I was terrified that she or my parents would find out. I just knew something wasn't right with me, and I felt ashamed. As I grew up, I became painfully aware that my fantasies were a dead end and that I would need to keep them a secret or they would ruin my life. For the most part, I was able to do this. No one knew about my gender discomfort. I was determined to have a 'normal' life, whatever that was, and if that meant acting like I was a man, I would do it—even though it felt very wrong."

Janet tried running at an early age, but it didn't immediately pan out for her. "I never really thought of myself as an athlete," she remembers, "because I didn't think I was good enough to be on a school team. I would have loved to be that good, and I did try to make it on my high school track team, but I was third string, so I quit and didn't come back to it until after college," she says.

Janet grew up in New York but relocated to the San Francisco Bay Area in 1969. It was there that she founded her company and discovered her deep passion for running. It started in 1972 with jogging around the neighborhood. Occasionally on her runs, she would see another runner. "I would come home and tell my wife, 'I saw someone else running today!' I would be excited about this because it was still so unusual. I felt like runners were members of a secret society."

The solo neighborhood runs led to her first race ever, the 1973 Bay to Breakers. Janet had heard that more than a thousand people ran all the way across San Francisco. She could hardly imagine so many runners. When race day came, she was thrilled by the crowd, eagerly anticipating a sprint across the finish line in an Olympic-like blaze of glory. But the race had doubled in size from the previous year, and the growth had taken the organizers by surprise. As a result, many people were bottlenecked at the end, and Janet had to walk the last half mile. "I decided the next year I would just have to be faster so I could get to the finish before the masses."

This was Janet's introduction to the world of competition. She loved the sea of people. It was a scene. "All these people coming together, like a tribe. It reminded me of the Human Be-Ins of the sixties, but it was a healthy tribe that was focused on fitness rather than drugs." After that disappointing first Bay to Breakers, she realized she needed a strategy. "I brooded for a whole year about walking across that finish line." The next year, she trained much harder, and at the end of her second Bay to Breakers, despite another surge in entrants, she got her sprint finish.

That was it. She was hooked.

During the next seven years, Janet kept running and kept making more discoveries about the world of runners. But things really changed in 1980, when she found out about the Tamalpa Runners, a group that today is one of the oldest and largest running clubs in California. Within a year, she was president. "I didn't really get carried away with running until I joined the club," says Janet. "Then it all happened quickly. I started running hills and training more seriously. Before that, there had been a time when I couldn't believe people would actually voluntarily run up hills when they could run on the flats."

Through her thirties and forties, Janet raced regularly and ran every week with the Tamalpa Runners. By the time she was approaching fifty, she was no longer at the peak of fitness but was still a strong male runner. Her lifetime personal records—a mile in 5:05, a 10K in 36:27, and a marathon in 3:01—didn't seem so distant. She still ran every Saturday and Sunday morning, rain or shine, with a group that consisted mainly of men from the club. They pushed hard, egging each other on anywhere from eight to twenty miles around Mt. Tamalpais.

In addition to serving as president of the Tamalpa Runners for fifteen years, Janet also edited and wrote much of its newsletter. Along with many of her Tamalpa friends, she was a Dipsea Race fanatic, always making the century-old, seven-mile cross-country run the centerpiece of her racing year. As of this writing, she has run twenty-five consecutive Dipseas—something she is very proud of.

"When I joined the running club, I started getting more committed to serious training. But it's not just the running, it's everything around it. I'm not going to say that we always have deep conversations when we run because, obviously, we are running, but there are real friendships that have come out of my running group."

In the club, Janet was regarded as a quirky, quiet, highly intellectual guy whose dedication to the group was well respected. This drew people to her, such as her best friend over the last twenty-five years, George Frazier.

"What I liked about Janet was that she read a lot and so she could talk about obscure topics for hours. And as busy as she was with her business, she always had time for a run. Running was a huge priority for her. One of the things that has always been true with Janet's running is that you always got one hundred percent in every run and every race. There's no quit in her. I no more than boasted once that she would never beat me, and then it always happened. Janet was able to keep me honest," says George.

George has been one of Janet's regular running partners for almost as long as they both have been running regularly, although he admits there was about a year during Janet's transition when their friendship was on rocky turf. When Janet first began to make her transition, she told George early on and then gave him time to prepare before she invited him over to see her as a woman. "There was a period where I had painted toenails, and I would be very careful about changing my shoes in the car because I didn't want anyone to know, not even George. Around when the time came to tell him, I started to let little things like that slip," says Janet. As she had suspected early on when she had hid things, this was tough for George to accept, in spite of being forewarned discreetly through little hints—like the painted toenails. Eventually, when he was told outright, he was not ready to see his running buddy go through this.

"It was very scary to me at first. I thought my best friend was going to die and this new person was going to take over. My loyalty was to my friend, not to Janet. The reality is, though, that Janet is still my best friend. We talk about the same stuff as we did when Janet was a man," says George.

George had attributed Janet's odd behaviors for a man—like growing out his hair in his late forties and painting his fingernails and toes—to her being in a rock band and part of "that" scene. Janet played bass with a group called the Finish Line along with several other musically inclined runners.

Janet remembers, "It was funny, because over the years, there were occasional evolutions to the social norms that I really enjoyed, and they let me feel a tiny bit more feminine. Like when it became okay for men to have long hair in the sixties, or when men started wearing Lycra running tights in the eighties. By the nineties, long hair on men was again out of fashion, so growing out my hair again was a big step. These funny little things really have nothing to do with femininity, but for me, they brought a secret, slightly illicit pleasure because of their symbolic value."

□ □ □

In 1994, Janet's life took some surprising turns. First, she and her second wife split, and she found herself single again. Then one day, she signed up for America Online, and that night, she sat staring at the search engine box on the computer screen. She could type in any word in the world, and she typed "transsexual." Why she didn't type in "running" or "music," she isn't sure. But with the word "transsexual," she discovered websites filled with information, message boards where she could read posts, and chat rooms where she could talk to other people who had spent a lifetime experiencing the same feelings she had. And it was all anonymous, all private.

"Before the Internet, this was something I just didn't want to think about. I wasn't going to go to the library or ask for a book on transsexuality in a bookstore. I didn't want anyone wondering why I was curious about this. I didn't want to talk about it."

Eventually, the Internet led her to a support group in San Francisco. At the time, Janet had a girlfriend who she met in the Tamalpa Runners. After about a year of privately exploring transsexuality, Janet was able to get the courage up to talk to her about what she was discovering online and how it was making her feel. Fortunately, her girlfriend's reaction was positive, and she encouraged Janet to embrace what she was discovering about herself, even though it ended their romantic relationship.

When Janet finally braved her first support group meeting wearing women's clothes, she realized she would need a name. She thought only for a few moments before deciding on Janet, not realizing that she was making a decision that would stick with her for the rest of her life. "That night, it seemed there was so much to think about," she remembers. "The name was such a small thing at an instant when I felt my life was at a turning point. In retrospect, I wonder what the fuss was about, but at the time, everything in my life seemed so monumental and every step seemed huge. When I look back on how concerned I was at what everyone would think, how they would all react, it seems now like I worried more than I needed to."

Still, after that first hesitant public appearance as Janet, her life was never the same. Within months, she had made the fateful decision to proceed with a gender transition, and she began with taking the hormone cocktail that blocks androgens and adds estrogen. She set a tentative goal for completing the process with gender reassignment surgery by the end of the millennium. Still, this decision didn't come easily as she worried about everything from her family to whether or not she would be able to run with her club ever again.

"After many years, I had come to an accommodation with everything. I wasn't going to let it rule or ruin my life. I did the best I could to accept the fact that even though I felt like I should be a woman and that I identified on some level with being a woman more than most guys, I wasn't. Still, I was able to cope with that and work it into my life and not fret about it and go on living."

In order to maintain relationships, Janet started telling the people closest to her, one or two at a time, by sitting them down and explaining that something was going to change in her life and that she didn't want it to affect her relationship with them. Then she asked them to keep the news secret until she was ready to go public.

But the secret was hot and hard to keep. "Once fifteen people knew, a critical mass was reached, and suddenly, everyone knew. So there was no point in hiding anymore. It was really a great relief. I was tired of living a double life." In July 1998, months ahead of schedule, Janet came out to her mother, her sister, her son, her friends, and her coworkers, and she began living full-time as a woman.

□ □ □

In the beginning of her gender transformation, Janet was concerned that her post-transition race times might be so fast that they would attract critical scrutiny—and, possibly, unwanted publicity about her private life. "There's tons of information out there dealing with how your body will change and how you'll feel once you make the transition," says Janet, "but little or nothing on how your performance will change in athletics. I knew where I stood in the pecking order as a man. The question was, would I be further up as a woman? If I ran my male times as a woman, I would go from merely being good to being a national-class athlete."

In 1997, before starting on estrogen and long before she went public as a woman, Janet had made an anonymous phone call to USA Track & Field to ask what rules applied to transitioning athletes. She was told there was no formal policy on transgender athletes, but she could submit a written request for a ruling. She hung up, having no intention to write such a letter.

Six months later, after Janet saw her first race results, the question was moot. She had always considered any 5K over twenty minutes to be slow, so she was stunned by her time as a woman: 22:43. Her male speed had disappeared, and interestingly, she was now only as fast as a woman her age, in similar physical condition, might be. In fact, she ranked within the same percentile that she did as a man: 74 to 76 percent. Because of the effect of the hormones, she had gained no advantage.

"When I ran my first race as a woman, I was shocked at how slow I was because I'd imagined myself suddenly setting the roads on fire. I assumed I'd be a fifty-something-year-old woman running at a national-class level. But that wasn't the case at all," Janet says, laughing. "No one tells you how your running times will drop."

"It was a bit disappointing to lose so much hard-earned speed so quickly," Janet admits, "But at least it meant I had no worries about being too fast. I was too slow to cause any controversy. As a woman, I have to work just as hard as ever to stay in peak race condition. And it became quite clear that once you have gone through the hormone program, you have no particular advantage over any other woman of your age."

The effects of steroids (male hormones and their derivatives) on men's athletic performances are well documented, and of course use of these steroids is illegal in competition. Yet currently there are no scientific studies on the performance of a man taking estrogen. What information exists is purely anecdotal, but it seems estrogen and androgen blockers confer no advantage and in fact lead to decreased performance.

In May 2004, the International Olympic Committee passed a ruling that transgender athletes could take part in the Olympics provided that their transition had been complete for two years. (This means hormones for two years, complete gender reassignment surgery, and legal recognition of their chosen gender.) "Although I'm an Olympic contender only in my dreams," Janet says, "I'm very pleased to see this long-overdue recognition that transsexual athletes have the right to compete in their chosen gender and have no advantage over nontranssexual athletes, as long as reasonable conditions are met. This puts an end to intrusive and degrading chromosome testing and removes any doubt about the right of people like me to compete at whatever level we can."

Looking back now, Janet considers that first 5K race as a woman to be pretty good—in fact, she never again ran that fast. But even though she saw her times drop, she still had some worries. One day, she approached fellow Tamalpa Runners club member Shirley Matson to express her concern that people might say their club was cheating because they had a transsexual running on their women's team. Janet didn't want to cause any trouble and thought perhaps she shouldn't run with the women.

Shirley chuckles when she remembers it. "I told her, 'Of course you should run with us! You're a woman now, aren't you? What else would you run as? I'll still beat you, anyway.'"

Every year, Janet runs against Shirley in the Dipsea, which is handicapped by age and sex. While Shirley, a four-time winner, uses visualization techniques to help her succeed, Janet only dreams about a high finish. She has no illusions of Dipsea glory. That said, in regular masters races, Janet has had better luck in picking up age-group wins than her male alter ego. This is not because of speed but because as the age group increases, the number of competitors decreases more sharply for women than men. "I don't know why, but more women seem to drop out of competition once they turn fifty," Janet says. "The men are still mixing it up right on through their sixties, but often I'll find that while there are loads of women in their fifties out there who could beat me, they aren't showing up at races. That leaves the field wide open for an average-to-good runner like me."

Janet still trains hard with a weekly track workout and a weekend tempo run with a group that's faster than her. For most of the people in their group, the tempo run is their "long, slow day," but for Janet, it's speedwork. She can only maintain contact with the group by pushing herself. She can't stop at a drinking fountain or chat lightly when she runs with them. She needs to conserve every ounce of energy to keep up, perhaps because of the muscle mass she's lost. "It's so hard to keep up with the gang. I guess anybody who gets older gets slower too, so everyone deals with this on some level. It's just that my speed dropped so dramatically in such a short time. Most don't experience that."

Every year, George organizes an annual pre-Dipsea training run. It's a fourteen-mile grind up and down Big Rock, Marin's second-highest peak, and although Janet used to make it to the summit with the main pack, these days, she makes it as far as she can and turns around once the crew starts running back toward her. This is hard for her, and she's quick to admit that losing her speed is the one thing she misses most about her former life.

I was always a competitive person," says Janet. "I am almost as competitive as I was when I was a man. I am just competing with different people now, but I still want to do as well as I can. I think for some transsexuals, they lose their competitiveness, but then again, maybe they were never competitive. When I look back on it, that's something I took with me from my male life. There are some other things too, though, like I still enjoy browsing hardware stores. I've learned that I don't need to be a clone of some traditional female notion. I am what I am, and I am okay with that. I am happy that I don't have to keep my life a secret and that I can be open about it. It was really a drag having a secret to carry around like that."

The other thing that hasn't changed for Janet is the social aspect of running. She would rather run a short run with a friend any day than a long run alone. "I would never make it as a swimmer because I couldn't carry on a conversation. I love the social aspect of running."

So what would happen if Janet couldn't run at all? "I would walk," she says without missing a beat. "For me, running is more about being with people. Even if I am injured and can't do a weekend run, I will still show up and meet everyone for coffee."

While Janet says running is social for her, it's also clear that it has been her identity and her therapy for nearly thirty years. It has also been one of her most loyal friends. And the way she explains it, it's easy to understand why running has become such an integral part of her. "When I am running, I am just running. The rest of the world just goes away. It doesn't matter who I am or what I look like," she says. "It's amazing how when you are focused on a sport you can close every thought out of your mind."

Chapter Six: Fifty Thousand Miles and Going Strong

There are very few people who can claim that at one point in their lives, they were among the fastest runners in the United States. But Shirley Matson can. And with the 1,970 records she has set, this sixty-five-year-old legend has become source of inspiration for runners of all kinds.

Shirley's running achievements are vast. She has covered 50,000 miles and has competed in 400 races, with 350 first-place victories as a master runner. She has won the famed Dipsea Race not just once but a record-breaking four times.

The start to Shirley's running career was actually pretty ordinary. In 1970, at the age of thirty, she was living in Oakland and had a boyfriend who often ran around Lake Merritt. She was curious about it, and he advised, "Just go out and start walking, and when you feel like it, run a little, and when you get tired, walk again. Alternate walking and jogging. You will be walking less and running more, and soon you will be able to run three miles around the lake."

The next day, Shirley put on a pair of Keds (she didn't own running shoes yet), went down to the lake, and started to walk and jog. "It was very measurable in the beginning because I had this three-mile lake to run around. I could tell every day if I ran farther and walked less. I don't know how long it took, but finally I could go around the lake. It became a routine, and I loved it." It was about six years later that another boyfriend encouraged her to run in a 5K women's race around Lake Merritt. "A race? What's a race, and why would I want to do that?" she remembers asking, and then, "How do you do that?"

Although she was very active—with skiing, tennis, swimming, biking, hiking, dancing, and teaching fitness classes—Shirley had never been a runner. But suddenly, there she was, standing at the start line and surrounded by two hundred women. The trail around the lake was a single track, and at five feet two inches and 102 pounds, all Shirley could think was, *I better go fast, or I am going to get trampled.* The gun went off, and that's exactly what she did—she ran fast.

"I went out like a rabbit, not knowing what to do, and about a hundred yards down the trail, I was gasping for air," she recalls. "I was in front, but when I looked back, there was this gang of women coming. I eased off, and everybody else seemed to be doing the same until about halfway around the lake. One girl came easing past me, and I thought, *I wonder if I can stay with her, and even catch her."*

At the time, Shirley didn't know the terminology for road racing. Things like "split times" and "kick" were certainly not in her running vocabulary. The mere fact that she was racing was such a novelty to her, yet it got her competitive juices flowing. Despite her ignorance of the terminology, she instinctively put on a "kick" to the finish and placed second overall in the 5K, with a time of 19:37.

She was so taken with running that the very next day, she entered a 10K race called the Golden Gate Charity Race. It started in Marin County at Fort Baker, went across the Golden Gate Bridge, and ended on the Marina Green in San Francisco. Because she had never run more than three miles, she was nervous that she might not be able to complete the race. She decided to start in the back of the pack of 1,200 runners to learn the lay of the land. Running slowly up the hill to the bridge, she began to cruise past other runners while trying to spot other women. "Where are they? Oh well, they're either way in front of me or way behind," she said to herself. After finally spotting a woman ahead, she put on a spurt of energy to catch her. Shirley said to herself as they sprinted toward the finish, "No way is she going to beat me." She didn't. With a time of 41:29, Shirley placed second woman overall in her second-ever race.

"Running felt good to me from the start," she says. "I liked the feeling in my body as I got toned. I had always liked movement and freedom. The simplicity of the sport, of simply putting a pair of shoes on and going out into the fresh air, just fit my personality I guess. If I had to live my life over, I would have been a dancer, but it didn't go that way. Instead I found running. And in some ways, running is similar to dancing.

There's a rhythm to it, and a discipline."

While she still wouldn't have classified herself as a "runner" in those first two races, what she did see was that she had a competitive spirit. She enjoyed picking a woman out of a sea of men in a race and then gaining on her and overtaking her. So she kept running and doing well, but only occasionally winning.

In the late '70s, Shirley moved to San Diego to work at the famed Golden Door Spa as a fitness instructor and nutritionist. She entered a few races at the encouragement of friends, and her times were close to the top runners in her age group. After turning forty in 1980, she made a decision to devote more time and energy to running, "to see how good I could get." She was inspired by and in awe of the top masters (over the age of forty) woman in San Diego, Dorothy Stock, who was running 10Ks in thirty-eight minutes or less—about a 6:30 mile. Shirley set a carrot for herself to one day beat Dorothy, feeling that if she could do that, she would have arrived as a runner.

In May 1981, at a 10K race called the Natural Lite Hypertension, she won in the women's 40–44 age group and met the top male master runner in San Diego, Dan McCaskill, Jr. He was impressed with her time of 41:20 and thought she had potential to become a top runner in San Diego, even nationally. "Dan gave me inspiration, motivation, guidance, and confidence," says Shirley. "Having someone truly believe that you can do it gives you the confidence to trust your instincts and try your best. I learned that I could set goals, be focused, do the hard work, and achieve personal satisfaction from my own efforts, regardless of the outcome." Under Dan's tutelage, Shirley's times started dropping, and at the October 1981 Run for Health, she ran a 10K in 38:53, beating Dorothy Stock by three seconds.

Though Shirley thrived on the competition of the race, the real satisfaction was in achieving her goals. On her forty-first birthday, she ran a personal best 10K in 38:28. This was the beginning of what Shirley considers her lifelong love affair with competitive running. In 1982, in San Diego—without any awareness of what the records were or who held them—she ran the Coronado Half Marathon in 1:20:48, setting a record for the women's 40–44 age group. Interestingly, some of her best times came after the age of fifty, when she even set three personal bests. She ran the Carlsbad 5000 (5K) in 17:27, the Jacksonville River Run (15K) in 54:33 (now called the Gate River Run and taking place in Jacksonville, Florida), and the Stockton Cal-10 (ten miles) in 1:00:24.

With record-setting times in the masters division for track came national recognition and the opportunity to travel to major races and compete with the top runners from all over the United States. Fellow runner Barbara Miller started competing in the mid-'80s with Shirley. Although Barbara lived in Modesto, she often came across Shirley at various races around California. "She is the best of the best," says Barbara. "When she is there, I am going for second place. Not because I give up—it's just the fact that she's so very good. Shirley is a fierce competitor, but she's also warm and supportive. When I do well in a race and she's not there, I often get an email from her, congratulating me on my performance."

Not only is Shirley a firm believer in treating everyone as well as you can at a race, she also believes a good competitor should look her best too. "My attitude at a race has always been that if you look your best, you are going to perform your best," she explains. "If you're all grungy and feeling kind of sloppy, you are going to behave and perform that way. So I would always put on full makeup—you know, lipstick and mascara, the whole bit, even hair spray. It's as if I'm going to work. After a race, people would ask me, 'Did you even run? It looks like you just got out of the beauty department.' On the start line, it's a psychological ploy. I like the dichotomy that you can be really aggressive and athletic and flirty and sporty, and still be feminine. Why shouldn't you be able to do all of that at the same time?"

Sportswriter Mark Winitz, who has written about running for thirty years, said that in many ways Shirley is the ultimate athlete, and that at the same time her mannerisms are not those of someone who is at the top of the pack. "Not only is she a superb athlete, but she's also a really personable individual and almost always available to talk. She's not just focused on herself, she's about the other runners in the race. She always talks about them with respect and how big of a challenge it was running against them and how well they did. She mentions invariably how difficult the day was, so it's not all about herself. It's a rare competitor who can do this."

Every year in December, USA Track & Field (USATF), the national governing body for running, selects Athletes of the Year. For thirteen years, Shirley has been awarded Runner of the Year for Long Distance Running for women in her age group. *Running Times* magazine has named her Age Group Runner of the Year seventeen times, and she was named USATF Masters Track Runner of the Year three times. She was inducted in the Masters Hall of Fame in 1998 and the Senior Athletes Hall of Fame in 1993.

"It's hard to believe that this many years has passed since I first starting jogging around Lake Merritt," she recalls. "I never thought I would be doing this thirty years later, but life goes on while you're living it. I've dominated the sixty-year-olds, the fifty-year-olds, and it really all started in my forties. It's hard to believe because I never felt like I was athletic when I was growing up, and here I am."

One of Shirley's favorite local wins is probably the Dipsea, which is on her home turf in the San Francisco Bay Area. If Boston is the pinnacle of road races for many runners, the Dipsea—one of the oldest trail races in America—holds the same fascination for cross-country and trail runners. It's considered one of the most scenic trail races, but it's also one of the most grueling, because the first four miles are uphill. First organized in 1905 by the Olympic Club, the 7.1-mile run starts in Mill Valley and sends runners up and over 1,300 feet of Mt. Tamalpais, then down to Stinson Beach. Like many distance races, the Dipsea did not allow women to join officially until 1976. But unlike other races, such as the Boston Marathon, there was genuine concern that this race would be too hard for women if they hadn't trained for it. Even now, thirty years later, only 35 percent of the people who sign up are women.

The race is handicapped—start times are based on gender and age. And because of the various start times, the key to winning the Dipsea is knowing the course because there is more than one way to get to the finish line. Theoretically, anyone can win. But also, there is a penalty for winning. Winners lose handicap minutes for the next three years to make it harder to win again the following year. "There's no money, it's not a championship, and there is risk involved because of the terrain, so it's not a professional race. It's for people who love the course," says Shirley.

Shirley was fifty-one the first time she ran the Dipsea, in 1992. At that time, she had been racing competitively for fifteen years, but the Dipsea was a very different race for her. First of all, it was on a trail, and most of Shirley's experience racing was on tracks and roads. Before committing to enter the Dipsea, she decided to do a group training run to scout out the course a few weeks before the race. It was a Thursday evening. "It sounded like fun. You have this nice run with a salmon barbeque at the end, and you get to check out the course. I thought it would be just a nice, leisurely run."

The day before, Shirley had gone on a forty-five-mile bike ride, and that morning, she'd already been on a six-mile run, so she was a little tired, but in her mind, it was only a seven-mile run. How hard could it be? At 5:00 PM, she went to the appointed meeting spot, where more than a hundred people were assembled. Someone yelled, "Ready, set, go!" and they were off. They started climbing the 676 stone stairs in Mill Valley, then continued going up, ascending Dynamite Hill, Hogs Back Hill, and Cardiac Hill—the highest point. (There's still another stretch, toward the end, aptly called Insult Hill.) Shirley held on, running as fast as she could, not wanting to lose the pack because she was unsure of the way. "It reminded me of my first race in 1977," she remembers, "where I thought, *Oh my God, what have I done here?*"

When she finished, the race organizer asked how she did. When she replied, he said, "You could do better once you learn the course. And because of your age and handicap, you could win this race." It was the first time that "age and handicap" had a positive spin. After the handicap system was explained to her, she decided to give the Dipsea a try.

A few days before the race, the local paper touted Shirley Matson's predicted time and announced that she was favored to win. The previous year, at age nine, Megan McGowan had won it, thanks to her speed and the handicapping system. This year, ten-year-old Megan and fifty-one-year-old Shirley would start together. Shirley remembers the beginning of the race well: "We were stride for stride down the road and up the stairs. When we got to the top of the stairs, Megan pulled away, and I thought, *Oh, she doesn't know how to pace herself. But oh yeah!—she did win last year!* I didn't see her again until about the halfway point, and she was one minute ahead of me. I was impressed. She maintained the lead, and I couldn't catch her. She finished in an incredible fifty-eight minutes. I ran a personal record of fifty-nine minutes and was very pleased with my performance. I can proudly say that I was beaten by an amazing ten-year-old!"

The next year, in 1993, the players were different, as were the handicaps. Shirley's main competitor was Gabrielle Anderson, the 1984 Olympic marathoner, who could beat Shirley by two minutes in a 10K. But the handicaps gave Shirley a two-minute head start, so the race could be close. Being in the lead has its disadvantages. You don't know where your competition is or how quickly they may be closing the gap. You run as hard and fast as you can, and you don't look back. Shirley did that, and although Gabrielle gained a minute and a half, it wasn't enough, and Shirley won her first Dipsea in 1:00:34.

Over the years, Shirley has learned that for her, racing is 90 percent mental and 10 percent physical. Her first experience with this was at the 1984 Peachtree Road Race 10K in Atlanta. Cindy Dalrymple was the reigning national masters runner and was undefeated in seventy-five races over two years. Shirley never imagined beating Cindy, but the night before the race, Dan McCaskill, Jr., called and told her she could do it if she set her mind to it. Then she started to seriously consider the possibility.

"All night long, I visualized the race," Shirley remembers. "I ran it over and over in my mind. I lived and breathed the race and my strategy. My plan was to go out at a comfortable pace and monitor Cindy, knowing she would go out ahead of me. If I could comfortably maintain a striking distance, and if the gap didn't widen, I would attempt to close the gap at mile 5 with the intent to catch her at mile 6, then put on a kick to the finish. That was my only hope. That was my plan. I would not play cat and mouse, and I would not take the lead."

Shirley recalls the race in detail: "The gun went off, and Cindy took the lead. She pulled ahead about a hundred yards, and I was able to maintain the gap. But then I noticed Cindy looking over her shoulder, and I definitely didn't want her to see me, so I hid behind other runners. Everything was going according to plan, but I didn't know there was a big hill at mile 5. Regardless, it was now or never. If I didn't try to close the gap, I would have no chance of catching her. I dug deep, focusing on my goal. I was gaining on her. At the crest of the hill, when we hit mile 6, I was on her shoulder. It was déjà vu all over again, and a little voice said, 'Who do you think you are? No one has ever beaten Cindy!' But I was not intimidated, and I answered the voice with, 'I just have to do it.' With that, I put on the kick of my life, thinking my legs were going to give out and I would collapse in a pile, but in a matter of seconds, I crossed the line in 35:59. Cindy finished in 36:05. It was a major upset, and it proved to me the power of the mind." Dan was right. It was a mental game.

While Shirley's career has appeared to be an easy run the whole way to the top, like most runners, she has had her problems with injuries over the years. She has had sciatica, illiotibial band syndrome, plantar fasciitis, a stress fracture, and more. She now knows that postural imbalances and muscle compensations have been a major cause. She has had a severe case of Achilles bursitis, and as of February 2006, she had not run for six months. "I have had to think about that recently. What if I couldn't run anymore? I have come to terms with the fact that this might be the end of my competitive running, and if it is, then so be it. I have had a very good time with it all, and it has been a nice ride. When you get to the mountaintop, you may have to say, 'I made it, and if I never get here again, it was a beautiful view and well worth the climb.'"

Many people—including Edda Stickle, the Dipsea's race director for the last five years—consider Shirley to be a major influence on the growth of women's amateur racing in the United States. "Shirley has set a new standard for women in running," says Edda. "She really doesn't verbalize how she feels about it, and she doesn't brag.

I do know that she's proud of the accomplishment, but she's very humble. She has so much discipline that it's great to see her come across the finish line first." Shirley was inducted into the Dipsea Hall of Fame in 2002.

While racing has been important to Shirley over the last thirty years, and while winning races like the Dipsea has been an honor she could have never imagined, it's still only part of why she loves running. More than anything, she's found that running has become her consummate companion. "Running is like my best friend because your best friend is always there for you, and understands you and knows you," says Shirley. "If I'm feeling joyful or happy, I can go for a run through the woods and feel that emotion. I don't need a lot of dollars for excitement. It doesn't cost me a penny to breathe the fresh air and run. Going through rough times is when I really love to be able to run. So running has not only been a sport for me, but it has also been a lifestyle and life partner."

"I started to run because it was fun and I liked the fitness benefits," she continues. "That's what kept me going. Along the way I found that running offered so much more. It gave me focus, purpose, challenges, goals, friends, travel, socialization, health, variety, and vitality. When I first started jogging around Lake Merritt, I had no idea what lay ahead, nor did I have a specific goal. I just ran because I loved it. It would have been impossible to imagine that one day I would become a national-class runner, set records, and have my name go down in the record books. I didn't run for the glory, the limelight, the Hall of Fame, or the Runner of the Year awards. Those were the consequences of following my dream. I did it for the personal achievement, the personal reward. I did it for myself."

Chapter Seven: The Leader of the Pack

At first glance, eighteen-year-old Sheryl Page seems like just a regular teenage girl. Her thin frame is apparent, despite the baggy sweatshirt and jeans she wears. She shuffles when she walks and looks down when she talks. She covers her mouth when she laughs and often uses a mere shrug of the shoulders as a response. She seems to struggle with putting together a sentence, with finding her words.

But Sheryl is not just a regular teenage girl: She runs fast. In 2004, she won the Oregon State Championships for the 1500 meter, setting an all-time record of 4:36. That year alone, she won six out of seven major events. And despite her young age, Sheryl has overcome plenty of barriers that had nothing to do with her training. She suffers from severe dyslexia and has trouble with her short-term memory. While no one is sure where these problems came from, some attribute it to poor nutrition in early childhood, as well as the fact that she grew up in a home where English wasn't spoken.

"Without running when I was younger, I think kids would have called me retarded with the problems I have. I can't read or do math very well. I learn differently, but so far, people can see past that, and I am accepted. I feel like I am a role model, and I can show people that you can have problems and you can overcome them," says Sheryl.

She was born in 1987, right before Christmas, and was the second of four children in a Mexican American family. Her parents had trouble with the law, and her father was in and out of jail for most of Sheryl's early life. Her mother died of cancer in 1994, leaving her children with their grandparents, who spoke little English and were very poor. Basic things such as proper table manners—how to eat in a restaurant, even how to hold a fork properly—were never introduced to her. In grade school, Sheryl performed poorly. But once the bell rang for recess, her special abilities came alive. "We'd have races around the playground, and I would always be up in front of the other kids," she remembers. "They would say, 'You're fast.' I just thought it was fun to run in the grass. I wasn't worried with how fast I was going."

It wasn't just the other kids who noticed her natural speed. The school's staff noticed too, especially one woman in particular: Vicky Jones, her sixth-grade teacher. In her years of teaching, Vicky had seen many types of students. As she saw it, Sheryl was, plainly speaking, the kind of kid who just slips into invisibility. So she was amazed when she recognized this wallflower from the back of the classroom—this girl who would sit, shoulders slumped, hair in face, never answering and never looking up—as the same girl she saw running so blithely outside.

In seventh grade, Sheryl joined the track team. All she had were some old shoes that were purchased at a secondhand store. They gave her shin splits, but that didn't stop her. Running helped her forget her problems—at least for a while. And she discovered another reason why she loved running: It leveled the playing field. Stylish clothes and grades (not that she had paid that much attention to either) didn't matter so much anymore when you were competing in sports. And she was good at running. When she ran people paid attention to her and praised her. This was something she didn't experience much in her early life.

As a teenager, Sheryl started to have fights with her grandparents, after which she would sometimes be locked out of the house, forcing her to spend the night on the street. Sometimes she would find refuge in the visitors area at a hospital, other times she would sleep under the bleachers at the track, and sometimes she would just run throughout the night. "With running, you are free to go wherever you want in your head, in your town. Sometimes I feel like I can run forever," she says.

Then, in 2003, Sheryl's grandfather passed away, and her grandmother was left to take care of all of the children by herself. It was too much for her. By that time, Vicky and her husband, Randy, had been helping Sheryl for nearly four years. Vicky had driven Sheryl to practice with a team in Boise, an hour away from where they lived in Ontario, almost weekly. Those drives started out silently in the beginning, but eventually Vicky was able to learn more about

Sheryl. "It was so easy to see that no one had ever come through for Sheryl. Her aunts and uncles didn't want her. Her grandparents were struggling with all of the girls, and then, when her grandfather passed away, that was too much for the family."

In 2004, Vicky and Randy offered to adopt Sheryl. Sheryl was hesitant at first as they were moving from Ontario, the town she had lived in her whole life, to a town four hours away, just outside of Portland. But eventually she accepted with the blessing of her grandmother.

"She's an amazing person," says her adoptive father, Randy. "She has this huge heart, and you can just feel it in everything she does. You can't help but want to see her life work out for the better because you know she won't take any of it for granted."

□ □ □

In the fall of 2004, Sheryl and her new parents moved to the western side of the state. It was the first time she had lived so far away from her sisters and grandmother—the only family she had ever really known. "I was nervous when I first got to Sandy High School, and I wouldn't say hi to people in the hallway," Sheryl remembers. "But then I realized that if I wanted to see any results, I needed to start putting as much effort into meeting people as I did into running."

So she joined cross-country and started going to practice—something she had never been very diligent about in Ontario. The team quickly warmed to her because she was such a good runner, and as she began to see that people liked her, she opened up more. And when she opened up more, she noticed something else: She was getting faster.

Paul Loprinzi—her assistant coach in high school and the main person who worked with her from 2004 to 2005—says Sheryl is one of the most incredible distance runners he has ever come across in his lifetime. "I don't know if I will ever have the chance to coach another runner of her caliber," he says. "She has been influential to all of her teammates. She is more concerned with others and their performance than hers, and she'll run her hardest so others will feel the pressure and be challenged to match her. It's amazing for someone so young to have such insight and to be so selfless in her running. She runs for the spirit of running, not to win."

□ □ □

On the morning of the 2004 state cross-country meet, Sheryl was a little nervous. Her coach noticed it, and as they got off the bus, he reminded her, "You have to believe in yourself, Sheryl. We do." It gave her solace, as did her favorite book, *Gerry Lindgren's Book of Running*. She carries the tattered paperback with her everywhere. As she was stretching, she reread a passage where Lindgren talks about his competitors being right behind him, how he could hear the sound of their feet and nothing else—not the crowd cheering, not the cars passing by.

The girls in Sheryl's heat lined up on the track for the 1,500 meter. Standing next to her was state champion Annelise Chapa, a runner who was rarely beaten. A few days earlier, Sheryl took a run and thought about what it would be like to win state, visualized how it would feel to cross the finish line first. The gun went off. In the first lap, Sheryl was behind the pack, and then she started moving up. Next, the pack separated, and she pounded through it. Soon she heard the bell signaling the last lap. "Right then," she remembers, "I thought about that part in the book where he heard the feet behind him and put on a kick. I did the same thing and picked up the pace and ran." With arms raised in victory, Sheryl crossed the finish line first, with Annelise just behind her. "It was the first time I truly ever remember believing in myself," says Sheryl. "I was so happy. I always wanted to have a moment like that, but I never knew that this would happen to me."

Until she won state, Sheryl never realized how much of an impact running had on her self-esteem and her perspective on life's possibilities. "I think if you are smart, you have to believe that you can never know your true running potential. You could go so far and for so long, and then one day something happens that's slightly different, and then you're like, *I could have run faster than that.* And suddenly everything is different. When I won state, I had that feeling. At first I didn't realize that I could break my other time and just run like that, and then out of nowhere, I had this feeling, and I *knew* I could just go for the finish kick. It's almost like you can't know how far your body can take it until you just go for it."

And as she's gained confidence in herself, her wins have continued to impress. In her sophomore year, she finished second at state in both cross-country and track. In her junior year, she was first in the 1,500 meter, and in the fall of her senior year, she finished fourth and is expected to place even higher in the spring of 2006. On top of her running, she was voted homecoming queen at her school. She also has a new job. But most importantly, she has moved into regular classes and is overcoming her dyslexia.

While her new life has distracted her slightly from running, her coaches don't seem concerned with this increase in social life. They see it as a positive benefit that will help Sheryl transform from a great high school runner to an Olympic runner if she sticks with it. "Sheryl loves to run more than anybody I have ever met," Paul Loprinzi says. "Kenyan runners will often run repetitions for hours and hours. Sheryl's work ethic is like theirs. During practice, I would tell her to go for a forty-five-minute run, and she would come back ninety minutes later. Or I would have her run intervals, and she would continue sprinting until she was satisfied and completely exhausted." Sheryl's passion is a powerful force, so he's had to find tricky ways to keep her from overdoing it. "Her recovery time is incredible, and she will ignore injuries—we'll have no idea until we see her limping," he says. "We almost have to force her to take time off to let her body recover because she doesn't like it when she can't run. She feels like it's wasted time. I have learned that if I want her to run easier the day before a race, I have to run with her—to hold her back."

This past cross-country season, Sheryl's coaches had her practice with the boy's team to make sure she was challenged enough. Teammate Brian Karsten remembers his first impression of her. "When you look at Sheryl," Brian says, "she doesn't look like this awesome runner. But she goes out there and does it, and her body transitions. She pulls it out of somewhere. She has this spirit where she just doesn't give up, no matter what."

Once, when Sheryl was still somewhat new to Sandy High, the two went for a run together during practice. The run was only an hour, but on that run, Brian learned about Sheryl's past. "It made me see how lucky I am to have the family I have. But with Sheryl, you would never know what she's been through. She's so optimistic about everything." According to Brian, Sheryl is the type of runner who gives it 100 percent every time. "She only knows one speed—hard," he says. On top of being impressed with Sheryl's tenacity, he and his teammates soon realized that her presence made their whole team stronger. "She's our hero," he says. "She makes us all work harder and want to do better, like her. She can usually beat about half the guys, and so it gives us all a push because no one wants to get beat by her. But if she does beat you, she still makes you feel so good about yourself. She's never negative, so it's hard to get down about anything around her."

Paul Loprinzi says that one of the things that distinguishes Sheryl so much from the other kids he has coached is that she's not competitive in the traditional sense of a distance runner. She doesn't brood before a race. She's friendly and wants to warm up with others. After a race, she seems happiest with herself when she knows that she's pushed others to their limits—that a rival pulled a personal record or had to throw up because he or she ran so hard. "Not only does Sheryl want to run fast, but she wants everyone else to run fast. She makes a race exciting."

□ □ □

A poster of Steve Prefontaine dominates the back of Sheryl's bedroom door. On a shelf, there's a trophy bearing a young woman with a ponytail. It looks a lot like Sheryl. There are more trophies and ribbons from her races on the shelf, and there's a closet on the other side of the room where she keeps a photo album that details her life. In it are pictures of her sisters and brother, her aunts and uncles, her grandfather and grandmother. There are also tons of running pictures. She is especially proud of one photo where she is leading a pack of runners through a trail in the fall. Orange and yellow leaves are all around them. It's a magical photo that captures a moment of freedom. "I love this picture. I just think it's so perfect, running on that trail, the way the light is. Can you see that?"

Sheryl finds a way to put words to everything she's feeling, even if it's in a very simple way. Her voice is always soft, and her handshake is even softer. There's nothing about her that's threatening, so it's hard to understand where she finds the strength to compete so fiercely. "As an exercise physiologist, I often rely on the science of running, but Sheryl has taught me that the heart is more important than anything," says her coach.

Sheryl's life has changed so much for the better in such a short time. That's not to say things are completely easy for her now. "It's hard for me to make close friends, but I like the people around me a lot. I think with my past it's just hard," she says. "Sometimes I don't feel like all of the other kids. I am getting better, because I know now I am a role model now, and that matters. I hope eventually I can be a coach and can help other kids learn that there's something out there for everyone, even if it's not running. To find your true goal in life is so important. Like me—I never realized how lucky I was to find running until later. Sometimes it's still hard to believe, but it's almost like a gift from God, and I don't want to waste it."

Word of Sheryl's gift is spreading. In her room on her desk, there's a stack of letters from schools interested in recruiting her. One of the letters is from Yale. Chances are they haven't seen her poor academic records, but it was still exciting for her to open that letter and see that a school so far away and prestigious knew she existed. But even if Yale did accept her, she's not sure she would go. It's ironic but true: When she's not running a race, Sheryl has a lot of catching up to do. Her plans for now are to go to community college in the Portland area for the next two years so she can continue living with Randy and Vicky. She's not ready to live alone. The world is still too big of a place for her, and unlike most eighteen-year-olds, she's just content to finally be home.

Chapter Eight: Going the Distance

4:45 AM: Wake up

5:00 AM: Eat toast and peanut butter or a muffin and coffee; answer emails

5:45 AM: Run for an hour with friend Susy Bacal

7:00 AM: Pick up around the house; wake up Jackson (her ten-year-old) for school

8:30 AM: Go swimming

9:30 AM: Grab quick snack; work in home office on the Tucson Marathon (she is the organizer)

11:30 AM: Run for an hour or more with Aspen (her dog)

1:00 PM: Work some more; drink a Diet Coke

2:00 PM: Run again

3:30 PM: Jackson gets home; have a snack

4:30 PM: Take Jackson to tennis or soccer

5:00 PM: Run for an hour

7:00 PM: Feed the kids (she and her husband have five kids between them, ages ten to twenty)

8:00 PM: Eat with Jim (her husband)

10:00 PM: Go to bed

Total miles: 15–20 miles a day; 365 days a year.

Welcome to the world of ultra runner Pam Reed.

"I don't watch TV, I never just sit around and do nothing. That's so hard for me," says five-foot, three-inch, ninety-seven-pound Pam. It may seem strange that something so simple would be so hard, but when you realize what this woman has done, it becomes clear that she has the energy of a rocket engine. Since she discovered endurance racing in her twenties, she has competed in five Ironman triathlons from Hawaii to Canada, run more than a hundred ultras, and raced in more

than a hundred marathons. In 2003, she broke the international 24-hour track record for masters American women by running 138.96 miles, and in 2004, she broke the 48-hour record for her age group (40–44) by running 220 miles in that time. In her spare time, Pam is the organizer of the annual Tucson Marathon and a mother to three boys and stepmother of two other boys, ages ten to twenty. To top it all off, Pam is a two-time winner—and the first woman winner—of the 135-mile Badwater, one of the most grueling road races in the world.

The Badwater is infamous among ultra runners. It takes place in July in Death Valley—one of the hottest places on earth—starting 282 feet below sea level and ending 8,400 feet above sea level, at a point halfway up the tallest peak in the lower forty-eight: California's Mt. Whitney. In this race the road can get so hot that runners have to tread on the white line to stop the two-hundred-degree blacktop from melting the soles of their shoes. Foot-size blisters are expected, as are heat stroke and dehydration. These are some of the enemies that runners fight as they trudge through the desert trying to tell themselves life is as cool as walking through a mossy forest in Oregon. Those who believe this hallucination may see the finish. The rest drop out.

But the biggest enemy of the Badwater isn't the environment. It's self-doubt. "If I were to have listened to other people and the limits they set, I would have never done anything. I certainly wouldn't have done the Badwater. I had friends tell me they thought I would die because it was too hot out there. They made me promise that if it got over one-hundred-twenty degrees I would drop out," Pam says. But she knows very well that it's not just other people who place the limits. "We all hold ourselves back," says Pam. "When I think about records I want to break, I can hear this voice in my head saying, *But you're too old*, or, *But you're a woman*. Who says I am too old? Why should my age matter? Who cares if I am a woman? What you have to do is say, 'You know what? I'm going out there, and I'm going to do my absolute best.'"

□ □ □

Growing up in Negaunee, Michigan, with a first-generation Finnish father and Swedish/Norwegian mother, Pam was a very active child and always had a strong will. In high school, she did ballet, tap dancing, gymnastics, and cheerleading. In college, she ran track and played tennis for Michigan Tech. During this time, the hardest thing for Pam was the fact that the other girls weren't as athletic as she was, that they wouldn't want to practice as hard and as long as she did. "They would skip a tennis match to go play flag football, so they could hang out with the guys. I didn't have many boyfriends, and I would get irate at these girls. I didn't understand why they didn't want to train."

Pam started running in college to help her stamina in tennis matches. She hated it at first. It was just a means to an end. But then slowly, over time, she began liking it more. One of the reasons was that it helped her control her weight—an issue that had been bothering her since she was fifteen. She suffered from anorexia through her late teens and up through her early twenties. After the birth of her first child, she checked herself into a hospital to deal with the problem.

"When I was in the hospital, they tried to convince me that my illness came from somewhere. They told me I must have been molested when I was a girl, and they would hammer that over and over into my head. I was never molested. I was anorexic because I was competitive and because I wanted to be as thin as this other gymnast—and then from there it became this challenge. I just decided the way to get skinny was to stop eating."

Pam awakened to the full extent of her eating disorder a few years later, when she landed in the hospital for a second time. One day, she met a woman who was around forty-five years old but looked eighty. She told Pam she checked herself in because someone told her they wouldn't force her to eat there. That was it. Pam was done. She swore she would get to the bottom of what was plaguing her and that she would never end up like this woman. Today, she still battles with her weight but realizes that food is the necessary fuel for her to run on a daily basis—especially to carry her through long runs. "The anorexic part is always going to be with me. It's not like I'm cured to the end all, and I never really liked to eat much anyway, so that's a problem. I have to really think about eating and make myself eat every day. But what I have really learned, through ultra running and especially doing races like the Badwater, is that I have to eat to keep moving. If I don't eat, I can't run. It's that simple."

Charlie Engel, an ultra runner who has competed against Pam, is an alcoholic with twelve years sobriety. He says that when he met Pam, their addictions were what helped them form an immediate kinship.

"We have demons in us, Pam and I. We use running as an alternative to our addiction, and while, to some people, what we do may seem crazy, to us, it makes perfect sense. It's just not possible to explain it completely. I think that our addictive natures are what drive us forward so hard and for so long. With it, we discover things about ourselves. With Pam this is especially true, and you can see it. She wants the discovery that comes with pushing one's own body past the previous achieved limits."

In 2003 at the Badwater, Pam and Charlie raced head-to-head for a number of miles, until eventually, Charlie couldn't keep up with Pam. Then in 2004, at the national twenty-four-hour track race, he was with her 90 percent of the time. They even chatted for a few hours. Then, in the final push, he lost steam. She kept on and won. The story of the tortoise and the hare comes to mind when Charlie thinks of Pam. Because of her shuffling technique, she may not look like an elite runner, but it's not speed she shoots for. It's distance, and she's the queen of it. "The thing about Pam is that she doesn't stop. That permeates every part of her life. She doesn't stop, ever. Her attitude is to stop is to die," says Charlie.

Later that summer, Charlie ran with Pam for a second time at the Badwater. This time, he used her pace—anywhere from a ten- to fifteen-minute mile. (It sounds slow, but when you consider a distance of 135 miles, "slow" is the key.) Charlie and Pam jockeyed for position from miles 60 to 110. Then he pulled ahead. He beat her for the first time ever—coming in third, while she placed fifth. "I owe that race to her. First of all, she made me cover my head up when I was getting delirious from the sun, and then, more importantly, she did what I could not do, which was pace herself well. So I followed her. She was the reason I finished the race."

□ □ □

Ultra running is, to put it mildly, extreme. Distances start at fifty miles and go up from there to one-hundred miles or more. Should the course be too hot or cold, too hilly or wet, you'll probably suffer, maybe severely. Though training and superior conditioning is of the utmost importance, many ultra runners will tell you that the most important thing is a tough and determined mind—and the ability to withstand pain. Pam ran her first ultra, the Elkhorn 100, in 1992 with her husband Jim. He hated it. She loved it.

People who have spent time around Pam when she races often say that her pain threshold is superhuman. She will push on with little shuffles in spite of agonizing pain. She knows it will pass. It always does. "If I paid attention to pain, I would never run. I am always in pain to some degree, and I feel like if I stop, it will get worse. When I feel a pain, I know if I keep going, it will shift to somewhere else."

"The first couple of times we did the Badwater, Pam never even looked at her feet or changed socks," says friend and crewmember Chuck Giles. "At the end, when we looked at her feet, they were hamburger. She would be going along and she would say, 'Ouch, I popped a blister.' She has the ability to fight through that kind of thing unlike almost anyone I have encountered. I have never seen her stop moving," he says.

In March 2005, Pam decided to rise to the challenge that another ultra runner, Dean Karnazes, posed in a magazine interview: to run 300 miles without stopping. With a few weeks of planning, she and her team came up with a 25-mile circuit in Tucson. Pam rested for a full four days, added a few pounds to her tiny frame, and beginning on March 25, she ran the circuit twelve times, for a world record run of 302 nonstop miles in 79:59:00. To the best of her knowledge, only one other person, John Gessler of St. Johnsville, New York, has run this far virtually nonstop, and he took a brief nap along the way. To keep her moving, a crew of friends and fellow runners took turns running with her every step of the way. She drank Red Bull and Ensure, ate a lot of oatmeal and pasta, and listened to her iPod, which her son, Jackson, loaded up with U2, AC/DC, Metallica, the Clash, and other energy-driven music.

Endurance isn't a sport for the young, mostly because it requires patience. And actually, Pam has used running to help her hone her patience as a mother of five sons. "When you are younger, you're going to go out like a racehorse. That doesn't work for this type of running. You have to be really smart and patient." Toward the end of the 300 miles, Pam reduced her speed from her normal ten-minute mile to a rate of almost twenty minutes a mile, shuffling along, doing whatever it took to finish. Again, friend Chuck Giles was there to help her complete her mission. "I wasn't worried she wouldn't make it," Chuck laughs, "but I was kind of afraid I might be ready to retire before she made it across the finish line."

Pam takes the ribbing in stride, as she knows her friends understand what she has achieved. "Accomplishing something like this is more mentally difficult than anything, so you just have to keep in focus and remind yourself that you know you can do this, that you're stronger than this, and to forget about that pain and how weak you can be. You need to tell yourself that you can do it. It's such a mental game to walk out the door and do whatever you have to do that day, whether it's a huge run or just going for a walk. I hate when I have doubts in my head, but I am not afraid to admit I have them."

Everyone has doubts sometimes, but not everyone knows how to deal with them. "The thing that limits us is ourselves," Pam says. "We tell ourselves that we can't do it, and we can't. I've run into that feeling in the middle of a fifty-miler, a hundred-miler, and in the three-hundred-miler. When I feel that, I just remind myself that I know I have it in me to do it. But it's what you go through during the time when you are questioning—that's what I want to help people get through and to understand."

When she is asked why she undertook the incredible challenge of running 300 miles, Pam has a simple answer. "First, I love to run. But second, I did this because I wanted to reinforce that historically women have had to do more than men to get the same recognition."

But the run wasn't just about showing the world a woman could achieve such a phenomenal feat. It was about tapping into the seemingly never-ending source of energy she has. Her schedule following the 300 miles is exhausting to contemplate. Ten days later, she ran the London Marathon; two days after that, she did a "double" Boston Marathon (that is, she ran from the end of the course the to beginning and then started with the rest of the marathon); and less than a month later, she went to France to run the Surgeres, a 48-hour-race that spans 178 miles. She placed fourth at the Surgeres, which was, to her, a major disappointment. At the end of June, she went on to the famed Western States Endurance Run, a hundred-mile trail run in the Sierra foothills of California. She pulled it off, but since she was thinking of it as a warm-up for Badwater, she feels as if she didn't give it her all. Two months later, she quit the Leadville 100 after mile 80 because she wasn't into it.

After months and months of training and racing, Pam's body had taken too much. "The thing is, I can quit. I know when I should, but it does wear on me for hours afterward. I'll try to analyze it, to figure out why I stopped. In the case of the Leadville 100, it was an accumulation of all I had done—and my goals were screwed up. I wanted to win that one, and that shouldn't be the goal. If you want to do ultras, the goal needs to be to finish a race, no matter how bad you do. Not just to win."

But for Pam, finishing a race doesn't mean it's time to rest. She runs 365 days a year. Even after the Badwater, Pam will get up the next morning and take a little jog to keep her body moving and her muscles from seizing up. It's this constant movement that seems to keep her in races long after so-called stronger competitors have dropped out.

But "stronger" is a relative term, and she is quick to criticize those who aren't impressed with all that she has accomplished. "I get really mad when people say, 'Well, not all the good runners were at the Badwater, so no wonder she won.' I don't understand what I have to do. I beat not just the women in that, but the men too. And *now* when I win an event for women, *that's* not good enough, because I didn't beat the men. Sometimes I feel like I can't win."

The criticism Pam has received isn't necessarily totally because of her running, though. It's because she unapologetically welcomes media coverage, and at the same time is openly vocal about the lack of sponsorship for women athletes. After her first Badwater win, there were grumblings throughout the ultra community that her win was a fluke. This made Pam angry. But instead of just getting mad, she just came back the next year and won it again.

Badwater organizer Chris Kostman explains that the root of the complaints came from the fact that the race happens in three stages to accommodate rules about gatherings in Death Valley because it's a park. Because Pam was unknown that first year, she was in the 6:00 AM heat. The last heat begins running at 10:00 AM, when the sun is blazing overhead. An early start is seen as an advantage and so the top runners are put in the third stage together. Pam's second year she started in the third heat and won the race again.

"I think most of us were surprised to see a woman win the Badwater that first year. It doesn't happen often in running. Her second win really proved that she had run it legitimately," he says.

Friend Susy Bacal has crewed for Pam on a number of races and runs, including the Badwater. Every race, Susy says that she'll go through a period of time where she and Chuck Giles think they could do the race, that it's not so bad. And then, at the end, their feeling is always the same: no way. "What Pam puts herself through is amazing," Susy says, "and not many people have the strength and mind to do what she does. I get so angry when people criticize her because they have no idea what she goes through to finish one of these races."

Pam tries to be thick-skinned about the criticism, but she can't help but hear it. It's undeniably what encouraged her to take on the 300-mile run. Since then, she's appeared on *Late Night with David Letterman* and *60 Minutes* and was featured in *Outside, Runner's World,* and *Marathon & Beyond.* "My kids wonder what all the hype is around me because they see the nitty-gritty at home. The bad stuff, you know. I yell at them, I yell at my husband. I know I am high-strung. I don't want to come across as a saint, and I want it to be clear that all of this running, it's not an easy thing. It's not easy for my family or for me. It exponentially adds to my stress level."

Whether it's because of her vast reservoir of energy, the hoopla around her achievements, or the fact that she has to juggle being a mother and wife with it all, Pam lives in a state of heightened vigilance. "If there's anything I want to be in life, I want to be honest with myself. I don't want to bullshit myself through anything. I know a few things to be true—like that I love running more than anything."

Chapter Nine: See Jane Run

Twelve years ago, Lori Shannon, a computer consultant living in New York City, decided to run a marathon, and so she told her friends. They thought she was crazy. They didn't say why, but she knew what they were thinking. Lori is the first to admit that she doesn't look like the stereotypical marathoner. She's five feet three inches tall and wears a size 16. She's been this size for as long as she can remember. But she didn't let herself get railroaded by her friends' doubt. Instead, she went to an athletic apparel store to stock up. The salesperson looked her up and down, raised his eyebrows, and said, "*You* want to run a *marathon?*" Little did she know at the time, but this question would launch her new career.

"My goal is to have every woman—whether she's sixty and has never exercised, or a sporty eighteen-year-old—feel comfortable and taken care of when she walks into our store," says Lori, who is now the founder and president of See Jane Run, a chain of Bay Area stores that cater specifically to women's running needs.

□ □ □

Lori grew up in rural Vermont and was always athletic. She ran on her own and rode a bike, and eventually, she started playing rugby. She feels fortunate in that for as long as she can remember she had somewhat of a fitness base—unlike a lot of the women who come into her stores. Still, she had to work at it, as it wasn't at all a part of her upbringing or her family's interests.

"I started running in high school in the late seventies, when running wasn't cool—and it certainly wasn't cool for chubby girls," says Lori. "It wasn't until I was in my late twenties that I decided to run a marathon. That whole process just completely changed my life and empowered me in a way that nothing else ever had."

For years up until she ran the marathon, she would go and cheer people on from the sidelines. At the time, she couldn't run more than a few miles, but after watching all of the people of all shapes and sizes running the marathon, she realized there was no reason she couldn't do it too. "Just watching the marathon got me more and more motivated about it. I started to think, *I could do this.* I think the most difficult part was my own self-image. I could never connect the dots between who I was and someone who could run a marathon. It was kind of a long process for me to realize that I could be one of those people."

That year, she convinced a friend to sign up for New York Road Runner's Club with her. She wanted to undertake more serious training. If joining the club was a difficult step, registering for the 1993 New York Marathon proved to be even harder. But once she was committed, it became a mission for her. After months of training, Lori ran 26.2 miles and crossed the finish line at 5:03. Since then she has run six more marathons (with a personal best of 4:38), completed three triathlons, and cycled across the country. Now she's strongly considering an Ironman. But it was that first race that changed her world.

A few years later, Lori challenged herself again. She had dreamed about riding her bike across the country, from ocean to ocean. She heard about a group going that she could join and signed up. It took them forty-two days, and they averaged eighty-eight miles a day. The ride was tough, but the first roadblock actually arose before the trip even started—when Lori went to look for a bike and clothing for the cross-country adventure. "It was just totally annoying, because I'm five-foot-three, and to find a bike that was built for my size was just a nightmare. I also couldn't find clothes in my size, and I felt like people were so incredibly condescending in the bike shops. By the time we started the trip, I was just fed up."

Before the trip, she and a friend came up with a plan to start a sports store that catered to women. She started taking business classes to prepare for it. The long 2,600 miles across the country, from San Diego to Ft. Lauderdale, gave Lori time to dream up the fantasy plan for the perfect shop. While her initial idea was to create an all-encompassing sports store for women, she eventually realized that focusing on running might be the most effective way to get women into the store and involved in sports. "Running is so easy. Anyone can pick it up without a huge investment or commitment. So it made sense." But the company was not just going to be about profits. A big part of the Lori's vision was to start a training club in connection with the company, so that women who have never done anything competitive could learn how to set goals, and to maybe eventually do a marathon or triathlon.

With her business concept clear, she was ready to put it into action. She took more classes at a business-education center in San Francisco, and by late 1999, she had secured a location and was ordering stock. She opened her first See Jane Run in San Francisco in 2000 with just $12,000 to start. In October 2001, she opened her second store in Oakland, followed two years later with a third store in Mill Valley. Since its humble beginnings, See Jane Run has expanded into a successful $2 million a year company with a thriving new online business. But there is more to come. In the near future, Lori hopes to expand to Southern California and to move up the coast to Portland and Seattle.

The hardest part of Lori's almost six years of business took place from 2001 to 2002, her second year. Her first year was relatively easy, in spite of the fact that she opened during the first month of Silicon Valley's "dot-com bust." The recession had just begun, so she had trouble finding employees. Most people were still graduating college and stepping into tech jobs that paid $60,000 a year—not going to work in retail for $10 an hour. But these weren't problems she couldn't handle. She worked all the time, acting as owner, employee, janitor, accountant, and everything in between.

Then in 2001, right before she opened her second store, 9/11 hit, causing a second ripple of economic trauma in the Bay Area. She admits she was somewhat concerned about opening the second store, but she just knew she had to. "Doing this was terrifying to me. Starting this business was way out of my comfort zone, but opening a second store was way, way, *way* out of my comfort zone."

She wasn't just out of her comfort zone. In many ways, she was outside of her knowledge base. She laughs when she remembers the first store's grand opening. "It was April Fools' Day. We were racing around, fixing things up. We opened the doors at 3:00 PM, and a woman came in and asked for a pair of socks. At that moment, I realized I had no idea how to ring up a sale, because I had never worked in retail. I didn't know how to use the register. So I had to turn to my employees and ask them how to do it."

Lori's sense of humor has helped her to deal with the trials and travails of owning a business, and so has her running experience. "I parallel running a business to running a marathon," she says. "When you start out, you're really excited. You're cruising along, and you think, *This is going to be great!* And then you hit mile 6, and you start to realize, *I have a long way to go.* But you keep plugging away. When you're halfway through, you start to feel really fatigued, but you know that there's an end in sight. It was kind of like that the first year. Whenever things got tough, I always put it in perspective of the marathon. I would ask myself, *Where am I? Am I in the beginning, where it's exciting and new, or am I at mile 20, where I'm really done?* I want it to be done, but I have a long way to go, so I have to get into the endurance mode, and I have to focus. I have to put all my energy into one thing and keep it going, even when I am tired and don't want to go anymore."

While Lori's careful to pace herself and grow her business slowly, she's aggressive with the training-program aspect of it. In

2001, she started See Jane Tri with about fifteen women who had never before trained for a triathlon. To date, See Jane Tri has trained six-hundred women for triathlons. Last year, See Jane Marathon got off the ground. There were sixty women in the initial group, and the club is expected to grow to over one hundred participants in 2005. Every fall, the shop also sponsors the See Jane Run Triathlon, aimed at getting new women into the sport.

The programs have been tremendously successful. They are simple to join and help take away any fear a woman might have about undertaking a physical challenge. "We've brought people into the program who have gone from not being able to run around the track once to going on to competing in Olympic-distance and half-Ironman-distance triathlons," says Lori.

"The basic principle is that we really want all women to feel like they can do anything they want to do," Lori continues. "And it's not something I have to push. I just hire people who are enthusiastic and helpful and want to see other women succeed. We have sixty-five-year-old women walk into the store, saying they're running their first marathon, and our staff will start jumping up and down and doing everything they can so that the women know they can do it. I have women coming up to me all the time with tears in their eyes to thank me for opening the store."

Lori is a trailblazer in other ways. In 2003, See Jane Run put on a plus-size fitness fashion show with a company called Bumble Bee Fitness. The company has been an inspiration to Lori because the owner trains plus-size women for triathlons and marathons. "The story behind her company is that scientists pointed out the fact that according to the laws of physics, a bumble bee should not be able to fly. We all know they do."

According to the U.S. Department of Health's data for 2006, the average American woman was five feet, four inches tall, weighed

150 pounds, and wore a size 14. But many sports stores don't carry clothing that will fit the average woman, and so most women don't have a decent selection of fashionable exercise apparel. "If women are out there doing sports, they have every right to be looking good and wearing the right clothes," Lori says. "If you're wearing your husband's sweatshirt, you're not going to feel as excited that you're out there in the world doing this stuff. Looking good is important. We're women—we want to look good. I think that shouldn't be overlooked."

This means carrying a wide range of cuts and sizes—especially for that all-important requirement: a good sports bra. Lori has devoted a whole area of the store to bras, and she works closely with her staff to make sure they understand how to really fit a woman for a bra. One of her favorite companies over the years when it comes to bras has been Moving Comfort, a brand she credits with making huge changes in the women's market when it comes to acknowledging the wide range and shapes of women's bodies. "You can't have three bras—small, medium, and large—and say that's going to cover it," says Lori.

Last year, Lori was at an elite running conference where she was shown a line of bras by a leading manufacturer. After the presentation, she said, "You know, you're showing me all this stuff, but you only have one bra up there, and it's kind of a crappy bra. What's the deal with bras? Why aren't you guys getting into that market?" She recalls, "One of the guys got all flustered and then said, 'Well, bras are fickle.' I was like, 'Well, bras can't be fickle. Are you saying women are fickle?'"

□ □ □

Ironically, owning a running store means Lori has been running less in recent years, so she's decided to make up for it by running a marathon in June 2006. Right now, she's running fifteen miles per week along a scenic route that winds through the streets of San Francisco, beginning at Golden Gate Park and ending at the Panhandle. "When I am running, I don't necessarily feel empowered or strong," she says. "I am not a great runner. I don't run fast, and I don't look like a gazelle. But it feels good. The impact running has on my life over the long haul is a sense of feeling strong and empowered. For some, running comes naturally. For me, it does not. But I find that even though I have to work at it, running gives me endurance in everything I do. I can work longer, tolerate more and get more done than most people. And I like that."

Whether accomplishing a new physical goal or opening a new store, Lori has realized that her greatest tool for dealing with intimidating challenges is the faith she has in herself. "What I learned is that you get used to living in risk, and the more you do it, the better you get at it. And the better you get at it, the more risks you're willing to take. And the more risks you're willing to take, the more successful you can be. I think a lot of people don't trust or allow themselves to be outside their comfort zones, but the rewards are amazing if you allow it."

Chapter Ten: Running Free

In April 2005, horrifying news came from Pakistan. In a town called Gujranwala, hundreds of people from a conservative Islamic political party disrupted a girls' minimarathon, declaring their participation

in public sports to be un-Islamic. They attacked race officials with clubs and bricks, set twelve cars and seven motorcycles on fire, and smashed storefront windows. The violence just kept on going, even when police fired shots into the air.

Weeks afterward, in West Virginia, another shot was fired into the air—not to quell a riot but to start the beginning of a 5K race. At forty-two, Asra Nomani was there at the starting line, ready to race for the first time since high school. She broke into stride, saying to her friend Christine Arja, who is also a Muslim woman, "We are running this for all of the Muslim women who can't."

As she ran alongside her friend, Asra thought of the irony. First, her personal cause for running was women's right to exercise, but the race was officially called the Race for Men's Health. Second, Hajar—the symbolic mother of Islam herself—was a runner. Theoretically, had Hajar not run, the religion of Islam may not have ever come into existence.

According to Islamic history, Abraham took Hajar as his concubine when his wife, Sarah, could not conceive. Hajar gave birth to Ishmael. But when Sarah suddenly and miraculously got pregnant, Abraham banished his concubine and infant son to the desert. To save her baby from dying of thirst, Hajar ran a quarter mile seven times, back and forth, between two hills, Safa and Marwah, desperately calling for help from God. As she started her eighth run, water sprang up from the desert, saving them both. Soon, a tribe came and joined them. Thousands of years later, the prophet of Islam—Muhammad—was born into the civilization that had sprung from Hajar's strength as a woman, a mother, and a runner. Today, one of the rituals of the Hajj is to reenact this part of ancient Muslim history by running back and forth between the two hills, seven times.

Asra recalled her pilgrimage to Mecca, in Saudi Arabia, two years before, and realized there was yet a third irony. Since Wahhabism—the puritanical brand of Islam that Saudi Arabia practices—deems the act of running too immodest for women, only men are allowed to emulate the symbolic mother of Islam.

□ □ □

Asra was born in Bombay, India, but has lived in the United States most of her life. Her family slowly emigrated to the United States, one at a time, starting with her father, Zafar, who arrived in New

Jersey in the early 1960s on a scholarship to finish his PhD at Rutgers University. Her mother followed, and in 1969, Asra and her older brother, Mustafa, flew over to join their parents.

As a Muslim girl in a predominantly white and Christian community, Asra found it hard to fit in. Then, on one fateful day in the fifth grade, something changed. It was recess, and her classmates had gathered at the baseball field to race each other for fun. "I found myself pitted against a girl named Barbara Veasley," Asra remembers. "I was intimidated by her. She tormented me in the hallways, playing leapfrog on my shoulders and laughing." The two girls squared off against one another on the baseball diamond. They had to run in opposite directions around the bases, meeting somewhere in the middle. The first person to reach home plate was the winner. Whipping around the bases, Asra couldn't believe the results when her foot hit home plate. "I beat her. All of the kids cheered. It was the first time I ever heard anyone cheer for me or congratulate me. I took it in stride. I didn't know what to make of this victory. It was so accidental. But I knew it was monumental. I knew I wasn't going to win any popularity contests, but running gave me a window into my inner potential."

The next time Asra ran against anyone was at the age of eleven. Lynda McCroskey, a girl who lived up the street, challenged her to a race. Lynda, with her svelte physique and sleek long hair, was one of the most popular girls in school, and her confidence intimidated Asra, just as Barbara Veasley's had. Nevertheless, Asra accepted the challenge, and they lined up at a street corner. Other girls gathered to watch, and when they yelled, "Ready, set, go," Asra took off. The wind snapped in her ears. The sun kissed her cheeks. She widened her stride. And then she dashed across the finish marker, just beating Lynda McCroskey. Asra was shocked. But so was everyone else. Nobody ever beat Lynda.

In seventh and eighth grades, Asra joined the track team. Running became the one place she could rub shoulders with her classmates out of the classroom, and it made her feel like she belonged. As she trained and got stronger, she gained an appreciation for the discipline and focus required of a runner, and she even signed up for her first magazine subscription: *Runner's World*. Reading the magazine inspired her even more, and she started keeping a detailed running log to chart her progress. In the logs, she recorded the weather conditions, the distance she ran, her workout time, and the overall feeling of the running. From her earliest days, she untied her long black hair and let it swing in the wind with her stride. "Running made me feel like I was in control of my body. It gave me a sense of power," she says. "I felt total freedom."

In the summer, she was coached by a local runner, Bob Taylor, who inspired her tremendously. Bob shepherded her running team through weekly 10K runs and at the Junior Olympic meets. His wife, Cathy, was pregnant one season, but she kept running through her ninth month, and Asra was impressed by her might. "She was so amazing," she says. "She was beautiful and strong. She taught me at an early age that to be a woman, you don't have to be frail. You can be strong and powerful and in control of your body."

On the track, Asra was a good runner but almost never the fastest. She ran the 880, the 1-mile, and the 2-mile. She often got third or fourth place, and she did beat the top-ranked girl once—it was a one-mile race, and it was her fastest mile ever, 6:03—a time that still makes her smile.

One weekend, a cousin came to town and protested that she shouldn't be allowed to run. He argued that she was violating Islamic rules, that a woman running was too provocative—especially a woman wearing shorts and a tank top. But her mother and father continued to support her. "My parents knew that I was happy running. They didn't want to allow narrow-minded traditions to kill that joy," says Asra. "I cannot thank them enough."

For her mother, there was no doubt that Asra would keep running. "It made her feel good," she says. "It made me feel good, too, to see her running. It made her conscious of her health, and it gave her a positive attitude toward life."

Asra's parents understood the link between mental health and physical exercise. Growing up in India, her mother had jostled with cousins, playing badminton, running on plateaus, climbing into the valleys, crossing terraced rice fields, and exploring nearby villages. Asra's father firmly believes that everyone, male or female, can live a better life if they include an exercise that they love in their daily routine. "I wanted my daughter to be as strong as she could be—physically and mentally," he says. When Asra turned nine, her father had asked her mother to have her stop wearing dresses, saying she was too old to bare her legs. But when she started wearing shorts and tank tops to run, he didn't protest, because he considered it a part of the athletic regime. As a nutrition professor, he knew her running made her healthier by pumping more oxygen through her bloodstream, toning her muscles, increasing her energy, reducing stress, and even helping to metabolize calcium. He knew that fully covered women in the Muslim world usually weren't free to exercise fully, and they ran higher risks for bad health on many fronts, including vitamin D deficiency, which comes from not being exposed to the sun.

Asra's father drove her to track meets and cheered for her from the bleachers. She remembers one meet in particular when there was a downpour of rain. After the race, she wept from her exposure to the cold as her father took her frozen hands and warmed them with his breath.

Asra was often one of just two girls in high school who ran with the boys, and she sometimes beat some of them. This was in the early 1980s, and girl's cross-country hadn't yet picked up in West Virginia. Many of the guys were uncomfortable when girls passed them. Asra remembers one race in which was about to overtake a boy. But he started limping and quit before she could pass him. "I knew that was his ego talking," she says. It was an important moment for Asra. "I saw the contrast between the boys who kept running even when girls ran shoulder-to-shoulder with them, and the boys who couldn't deal with a strong girl passing them." This became a life lesson for her, and as the years went by, she continued to take note of how men reacted to strong women.

Running continued to remain Asra's passion throughout her late teen years. But just before the start of her senior year in high school, she developed chondromalacia, or degeneration of the cartilage, in her left knee. In those pre–arthroscopic surgery days, her team's personal trainer recommended aspirin for the constant nagging pain. This didn't help, and she had to give up her intense training. From then on, running was more for fun and fitness than for time. Unable to run cross-country her senior year, Asra threw herself into her other passion, journalism, working as an editor on the school newspaper, the *Red & Blue Journal.*

At West Virginia University in Morgantown, she first pursued a degree in chemistry but then ditched it to become a journalist. One summer, she interned by day at *Harper's* in New York City, and in the evenings, she ran the streets of Hell's Kitchen, in Manhattan's West Side, trying not to inhale the fumes of buses departing the Port Authority. During her last year in college, she started writing for a college version of *Newsweek.* After getting her master's at American University, she was offered an internship and then was hired by *The Wall Street Journal,* and her globetrotting career in journalism took off.

After the terrorist attacks of 9/11, Asra started to pay closer attention to Muslim fundamentalism, something she hadn't known a lot about even though she was a Muslim herself. By the end of the month, she was sent to Pakistan to cover the war on terror for *Salon,* and she set up her base in the port city of Karachi. Even though Karachi was actually extremely dangerous, at the time, most still believed that journalists were protected from the chaos in so-called safe zones—places, usually hotels, where journalists stayed.

Asra lived in a hotel for a few months at first, but she felt like a caged animal. Not only could she not run, but she could barely walk down the street without being harassed. She moved to a wealthy, sheltered part of town, where every other day she would do the unthinkable for most Pakistani women: She would lace up her running shoes, put on a T-shirt and pair of yoga pants, and walk to an oasis called Defence Park. Once in the safety of the well-guarded park, she would run laps around a quarter-mile track. "To some, I was nuts. To me, I was free," she says. It was Asra's only true escape from the intensity of the life she was living in Pakistan, and she clung to it fiercely. She never saw other women runners, only men. There were women who walked—"aunties," as she calls them. They were women in their fifties and sixties who wore traditional clothes that disguised their bodies. "It was walking on that busy street leading to the park where the general public was that I felt really self-conscious. Once I was in the park and running I felt safe."

□ □ □

In January 2002, journalist Daniel Pearl, a close friend and colleague from *The Wall Street Journal,* came to Karachi with his wife, Mariane, who also was a freelancer writer, and the couple stayed with Asra. One evening not long after their arrival, Daniel left for an interview with a spiritual leader linked to possible terrorism. He waved goodbye to Asra and Mariane, who was five months pregnant at the time, and hopped into a yellow cab. He never returned. He was kidnapped by a militant group called the National Movement for the Restoration of Pakistani Sovereignty, and they eventually killed him.

After Daniel's disappearance, Asra and Mariane spent every waking moment trying to find him. Four weeks later, Asra got some more startling news: She herself was pregnant. But her Pakistani boyfriend had walked out on her the day after Daniel's kidnapping, not wanting to get roped into the international dragnet, and when she told him she was pregnant, he urged her to get an abortion. In Pakistan, sex outside of marriage is a crime. Premarital sex is punishable by a hundred lashes; extramarital sex is punishable by death, usually by stoning.

Confused and scared, Asra phoned home and told her mother she was pregnant and didn't know what to do. She knew her mother would be accepting of any decision she made. In America, her mother refused to wear a scarf on her head and had rejected the parts of Muslim society that supported the oppression of women. "You are free," her mother told her. Soon after, an email came from her father. It said, simply, "I love you." This gave her the strength to make the decision to keep her child.

In the last week of February, after Daniel's beheading was broadcast on the Pakistani news, she returned home to Morgantown. But she didn't stay long—just long enough to see her parents. Then she quickly departed for Paris to be at Mariane's side until her widowed friend gave birth. Once Mariane's new baby was born, it was time to go back to Morgantown once again. Asra returned to her parents' house, both financially and emotionally broke, and started to prepare for the birth of her child. "My parents had a baby shower, and I felt like I didn't deserve it. I was an unwed mother-to-be. I was so depressed.

"I know I probably should have kept running all through my pregnancy," she says, remembering the wife of her high school coach. "And I always thought I would. The endorphins would have helped with the depression I was dealing with, but somehow I couldn't make myself do it." Then a social worker from the hospital gave her some advice. "You have to take control of your life," she said. "You have to be prepared for your delivery day. You cannot be in another time zone where the baby's father lives. You have to be here." This helped Asra snap out of her funk, and a month later, when her son, Shibli, was born, she was ready. "I was strong when I focused on his birth. I brought my son into the world, and he was beautiful. And it was then that I really started to believe that I could be happy and that I could decide where my next stride would be directed."

Asra had a cesarean section, leaving her body and mind feeling . like they, too, had gone through war. It took another six months before she laced up my shoes for a run. "It took me that long to feel like I was worthy of being powerful and strong," she says. "I healed in that year with the love of my family, my friends, and my community. And then once I started running, I felt so much of my strength coming back."

These days, Asra runs on the gently curving roads around her hometown of Morgantown, West Virginia, enjoying the serenity of her surroundings and the freedom running gives her. Her sense of inner calm, cultivated through years as a runner, has served her well. Whether as a journalist reporting from the Middle East, as a Muslim challenging Islamic traditions, or as a single mother raising a three-year-old son, a constant source of strength and inspiration comes from the miles she has logged. For her, running helped form a core of physical and emotional strength.

Not long ago, she was running a local four-mile run with her fourteen-year-old niece, Safiyyah. As they reached the crest of the hill, she asked her niece, "Do you know what power running gives you?" She wanted to impart to her niece a sense of the emotional value of knowing the strength of your physical strength. At that moment, they approached the crest of a hill, and Asra remembered the two approaches she had learned as a girl, facing the hills of West Virginia: look down, or look up. "Let's look up," she told her niece. "Our goal is ahead of us. Let's reach it." To Asra, reaching the summit was exactly how she had learned to approach the challenges that had come her way, from coping in Karachi to seeing her baby into the world. "I look ahead. I keep running until I get to the top of the hill, and then I look for the next hill."

Asra also often runs with her son, Shibli, who raced across the finish line with her when she completed her 5K in the West Virginia woods. Now three, he jogs beside her, regularly ponying up to imaginary start lines in bent-knee, sprint-ready position, finishing the annual Clarksburg, West Virginia, kids' run with Ronald McDonald, and stopping for breaks in the sand box of the long jump pit when the two of them run at the local track of Asra's younger days. In Pakistan, just before the one-year anniversary of the torched girl's mini-marathon, more than fifteen-thousand women and men in the city of Lahore ran in a marathon that has come to symbolize the battle between Puritanism and progressive values. Just as it is for Asra, runners said the victory was won at the word "Go!"

"Many Muslim women cannot feel the wind on their faces," says Asra. "They must cloak themselves from head to foot when they step outside their homes. In America, we have the right and freedom to this simple joy. I feel that joy every time I go running. It's an irreplaceable feeling."

Chapter Eleven: A Double Life

It's hard to imagine that a full-time schoolteacher and forty-one-year-old mother of four would have time to live a double life. But Anita Ortiz is full of surprises. On top of taking care of her

large family and devoting herself to her students, she has found a way to become a world-renowned trail runner, ranked as the eighth-best masters trail runner in the world.

From 2000 to 2003, she won all but four of the fifty events she ran in, and she earned the title of U.S. Women's Mountain Running Champion from 2002 to 2004. She was also the USA Track & Field Female Runner of the Year in 2002 and 2004 for the trail running category. In 2002 she made the USA Track & Field Mountain Ultra Team. From that point on, she quickly ran to her spot as the eighth-ranked woman in the world and the number-one masters woman in the world. (The masters age category for women in world competition starts at thirty-five on, and she got her number-one ranking at the age of forty). She has won the Pikes Peak Ascent (said to be one of the world's toughest races) four times, with a personal best and age-group record of 2:44:36.

Anita is just as surprised by her achievements as everyone else. Had someone told her ten years ago she would become a professional athlete, she would have laughed. She hadn't even competed in anything since high school: How could she end up a world-ranked athlete?

"I have had an uncomfortable dance with competition my whole life. I love to run, but I am highly competitive and so for a long time I just couldn't compete because I couldn't handle how nervous I would get and how racing made me feel. As I get older I have gotten better at managing it, which has allowed me to get out there and compete," says Anita.

As the youngest and the only girl in her family, she spent a lot of time alone while growing up in her suburban Colorado neighborhood. This led to her discovery of running in the second grade. "I was on my own, and so I'd get home from school and run around the house until dinner. I actually literally wore a track around my house by the end of second grade." She would dash around the back yard, where the "off-road" section was, come around the front of the house, jump over a bush, run across the driveway—and then start all over again. At dinner, she would proudly tell her parents the distance she ran. One day it was ten laps, then it would be twenty-five.

Starting in fifth grade, she did what she called "training" for an annual race day that would happen at her school. "I was really serious about it. We had this six-hundred-yard walk/run, so I would train by running home from school. I wouldn't walk home with any of my friends. My parents made me wear dresses to school until I was in seventh grade, so I was in my little frock and patent leather shoes running down the street." She based her timing on *The Brady Bunch*. If she made it home in time to catch the beginning theme song of the popular '70s show, she knew she had made good time.

In junior high, things changed. She started hanging out with the "bad kids at the corner" who smoked and nipped liquor from their parents. Running stopped, and fights with her parents started. "I was kind of a rotten kid," she admits. "I was trying to find my identity, but I didn't have anything to ground me then." But Anita's dad soon came up with an ingenious way to get her back on the right track—he started running. He would make sure to pass by the Taco Bell where she would be hanging out with her friends. Anita remembers the first time she saw her dad run by. He waved and smiled, shouting a friendly hello to her and her friends. That's when the guilt sunk in. "I was like, *Awwww, what's he doing? I should go run with him.*"

It worked. One day, Anita joined him, and running became a bond between them throughout the rest of her teenage years. Every morning, they would get up and go for runs together, but it wasn't until years later, when Anita had her own kids, that she understood the importance of what her dad had done. "Running helped me realize how much my family loves me."

When Anita was in high school, she joined the track team and was eventually offered a scholarship to college. But she realized that she had developed a love/hate relationship with competition, and she didn't like the way it made her feel. Her need to win had started to overshadow the real reasons she loved running—the ritual and the meditational aspects of it, the appreciation of nature—and she knew she didn't want that. So she gave the scholarship up. Now that she is racing again, Anita still struggles with her competitive nature today. Being a self-described type-A personality, she has constantly struggled with coming to terms with the fact that she might sometimes lose. "I really had to learn how to balance the nervousness of competition with the fun side," she says. "It was hard to tell myself, *Well, you're not going to win every race,* especially after winning so much. You get spoiled. And then you totally bomb out in a race, and it's hard. It's really hard."

After college, Anita moved to Vail, Colorado, where she started teaching at a local elementary school. A fellow teacher, Joy Ortiz, befriended her and soon realized that Anita's love of the outdoors would catch the attention of her son Mike, who was the race director for the Vail Recreation District. She skillfully set them up. "She had me picked out for a year," Anita says with a smile.

The matchmaking was a success, and Anita and Mike got married. As a race director, it was hard for Mike not to notice Anita's talent for running. He thought she should give racing another try, but she was still wary of the competitive aspect—in fact, she was worried the stormy relationship with winning and losing she had remembered from high school track might be even more pronounced as an adult. But he continued to encourage her, and eventually she agreed. And she did well, which is significant in Vail, Colorado—a mecca for athletes and the home of many professional runners, cyclists, and other outdoor enthusiasts.

Anita may have feared the strength of her competitive nature, but Mike didn't. One day, after a few local races had come and gone, he said to her, "You know, you only got fourth in that last race. What's up? You're better than that." Anita explained there was always something that slowed her down—an untied shoelace or the need to go to the bathroom. He told her to stop messing around: "So get your shoes tied beforehand, and go to the bathroom before the race starts!" Anita remembers this with a laugh. "He kind of ribbed me about it," she said, "and so I got myself more ready the next time, and I won the Piney Lake Half Marathon. I'll never forget that one!"

Mike's love and support continued to be instrumental in Anita's progress as a runner. When Anita first started racing, Mike called one of their best friends and fellow runner, Nancy Hobbs, who is credited with getting trail running recognized as a formal sport by USA Track & Field. "It was very sweet," Nancy remembers of the phone call she had with Mike, who was seeking advice to help his wife be a better competitor. "He really believed in her and wanted her to be successful, so he asked me all of these questions about racing, diet, training."

In addition to Mike's support, Nancy thinks that what sets Anita apart is her uphill climbing, which she is now known for. "She's incredible in the mountains. She has no fear when she is running and almost bounces like a deer when she is going uphill." Anita can explain what it is that drives her harder up those inclines: "I like running uphill because you have to run hard, give it your all, and check your gut at the start. Above all, never quit, and keep in mind that if you feel bad, everyone else does, too. I am mentally tough. That is the biggest part of the battle."

But as with many achieved runners, Anita has the tendency to overdo it. In 2004, she broke her foot less than a mile into a 10K race in Italy—but still went on to finish in eleventh place. Eventually, doctors discovered that Anita had completely ruptured her plantar fascia, and they said the injury was irreparable. (The plantar fasciae, used for pushing off the ground with your toes, are important in walking and running.) Anita was told her running career was over, and she was devastated.

But a few weeks later, a previous doctor of hers who had been treating her for various minor injuries over the years returned to the area and asked her to come in. He admitted the injury was bad but thought she could find a new way to run and could get back on her feet if she really wanted to. "Having that doctor believe in me made all the difference," says Anita now, looking back on that stressful time. She had high-tech custom orthotics made and learned how to run by pushing off the ball of her foot instead of her toes. This changed the way she was running entirely, but it worked. Downhill was hard, but uphill was pain-free. This continues to be the case today.

"Running with constant injury has actually in a way eased some of the pressure off of me in competitions," says Anita. "I used to think a lot about how I was going to manage pain when it came on. Now I just know it's there, and so I can focus more on just having a good race and not worry about when the pain will start."

Her injury, in spite of learning how to work around it, has admittedly still been tough on her ego because for the first time in five years, she isn't winning races she has easily won in the past. In June 2005, she placed tenth among women in the Teva Mountain Games Trail Run in Vail, Colorado. Even though she was on her home turf, it was just not going to happen that day, no matter how hard she pushed. She spent the last eight kilometers of the 10K race working out in her head how she would get through the loss. It was a big step for her. Her normal reaction to a mediocre race in the past had been tears and a feeling of total failure. But this time was different.

"It was just a blow, not because I didn't win, but it was more like, *Wow, how did that happen?* I was just surprised by it all, I guess. I spent a lot of that race working over in my head how to be okay and not get too overwhelmed by the outcome." She reflected on her life and what brought her to the point she was at in that race, and somehow, she was able to see past the loss. "It allowed me to look at the fact that racing won't be a part of my life forever, so I need to be grateful for the amazing time I have had and all that I have seen. I mean, look, I was this wife and mother. It's hard to believe all that has happened to me. I never would have thought this could be part of my life."

□ □ □

Since her injury, Anita has started using some devices to help remind her what running is all about. When she is doing long training runs, she always stops for at least five minutes in one spot to enjoy the view. This is hard for her, especially on the days when she's running late or has a lot of things on her mind. But she's learned that taking that five minutes to really appreciate the run, the nature, and her body ultimately helps make every run better. There are times when she will literally turn her stopwatch on for five minutes and not let herself leave that place she has stopped until the five minutes are up.

With this approach, Anita has been able to make sure she stays in touch with that aspect of running that made her fall in love in the first place: communing with nature. She doesn't always need to stop and smell the roses, though. She's able to lose herself even in midstride. "It's kind of scary," says Anita, "but I could just go forever when I run. It feels so good, like I never want to go back to reality. I just love being out, and I love the way things smell and the way things sound. I get caught up in the way things look and the shadows on the ground. Other than looking out for logs I don't want to trip on, I become pretty unaware."

"On some of my best runs," she continues, "I don't really see anything, and then all of the sudden, it's like, *Wow, I am already here,* and I won't remember getting there. It's kind of like this out-of-body feeling, where you don't feel your legs move, but you have this feeling of going and everything else is just not there. I love being in that place, and that's probably why I keep doing this."

Nature isn't always relaxing for her, though—in particular in the early mornings, when she runs alone in the dark on remote trails around Vail. She uses a headlamp until the dawn sets in, and she keeps her eyes on the trail. She's not afraid to admit that she gets spooked because she knows there are mountain lions and bears around. "I used to carry pepper spray, and then I saw this documentary. It showed how mountain lions attack at eighty miles an hour from behind. That's when I realized pepper spray is not going to do me any good. So now I have decided that when it's my time, it's my time. Still, when it's kind of dark and you have a headlamp on, and you look out and see a log, it looks like a bear. Or I'll see a rabbit's gold eyes and think, *Mountain lion!* But the longer I run, the less I think about that."

Anita has found another way to take the edge off of her competitive nature (and at the same time feel more protected from wild-animal attacks). Three times a week, instead of running alone in the dark, she runs with the Eagle Mountain Runners, a group she started with a few friends six years ago. Since then, it has grown into a group of fifty women. The runners take off in the dark of early morning at 4:45 AM, with headlamps bobbing in the darkness. These runs are easy for Anita, and she often leads the pack, and then takes another hard run later in the day to make up for it. But she wouldn't miss those early-morning group runs for anything. They feed her soul and remind her to have fun. "It's a good balance," says Anita, "and it works for me to have easier runs mixed in with my hard runs. Some of our runners struggle with three miles. But yet they go home feeling exactly the same way I do. They go home feeling proud of themselves, and strong and capable." Some of the members run regularly, some just occasionally, but Anita is the cement that holds the group together. She likes this role, and even though it adds another element to her already hectic life, it helps remind her why she runs.

□ □ □

Because of the support of both her family and the school where she teaches, Anita has been able to build a bridge between her lives. "The school loves it," Anita says, "because it teaches the kids about the possibilities that come with competition and traveling the world. And they think it's great that they can brag about having a world-class runner in their school." She brings back pictures and does slideshows to show them what she saw in the world, and her students love to keep up with her racing wins.

A few years ago, Jonny Stevens, who was in Anita's class as a kindergartener, saw a newspaper article about his former teacher, who was then racing in an international competition. It sparked his curiosity about the sport, and he called her for advice. Now, a few years later, he is a high school senior on the junior national trail running team. "It's such a neat thing that he knew about trail running through me," says Anita. "And I know a lot of my daughter's friends are into it, too, because of me. The kids get a kick out of it. Especially the older kids, who can kind of understand what it is I do. And I know there are some fifth graders that I'll see at school, and they're amazed at what I do. They say stuff to me like, 'You're so fast. I want to be like you.' I love it when they say that. It makes me so proud of what I do."

Anita's family is solidly behind her. During the summers, she and Mike load the kids and cart them around to Anita's races in the Rockies. If they have to go far away for a race, Anita's parents will take over and stay with the kids. But it's a constant juggling act. "My family is very proud. And I think it's very exciting for the kids. I don't know if they even know what they're proud of sometimes. They know that Mommy runs. I hope that when they get a little older, they can really put it into perspective and say, you know, "Mommy was the eighth-best trail runner in the world!"

On the wall, she has a pair of golden snowshoes, which her

children love to admire (on top of being a world-renowned trail runner, Anita was the 2005 North American Snowshoe Champion for the 10K distance). And in her closet, Anita keeps a box where she stores all of her medals and ribbons. From time to time, her kids pull the medals out to tell her which ones they think are pretty. "It's really important to me that they learn how important fitness is. I think that's part of why I run, so they can see me doing this and know that they can do whatever they want to do to. It definitely feels like it's given me a whole new enthusiasm about myself, and that translates into my family."

Anita is fortunate to have found a way to lead a double life and not be torn in half by it. The power that comes from being a champion athlete bleeds into her other lives—as mother, as teacher—making her stronger there as well. But despite the interaction among her various identities, Anita has been able to keep things straight. Yes, her love of nature and love of victory are two things that feed her desire to run. But there's something even more basic that fuels her. "For me, the biggest thing with running is that it empowers me. It gives me a sense of *Okay, this is mine. I make this happen.* I'm a mom because of my kids, and I'm a wife because of my husband, and I'm a teacher because of my school. But I'm a runner because of me."

Chapter Twelve: Beating the Odds

In 1998 forty-four-year-old Louise Cooper discovered a lump in her breast during a routine self-exam in the shower one morning. The lump worried her, but she decided to ignore it for a few weeks. She had other things on her mind at the time—namely, an adventure race in Ecuador that was coming up at the end of the summer. But every morning in the shower that week, she found her hand going to the lump. It eventually worried her enough that by the end of the week, she decided to see her doctor, even though she had an annual exam planned for the next month. The surgeon was certain it was nothing but fatty tissue but wanted to remove it anyway.

After the surgery, she was stitched up and told not to go running for a few days. But Louise had been an ultra runner for twenty-five years. To her, running was as important as food or water. So she waited a day after her surgery and then went for a run. "I ended up running sixteen miles with my hand on my breast the entire way," she says, "just to keep it from having any movement. Just a little security."

A few days later, Louise received one of the biggest shocks of her life. Rather than fatty tissue, the lump was diagnosed as a Type IV breast cancer, which has a mortality rate between 75 and 95 percent. The morning after her diagnosis, she woke up confused and scared. "I felt the world caving in on me, and I needed to do something normal so that I could ignore the fact that I, Louise Cooper, who had raced around the globe, battling all kinds of near-death experiences along the way, was now going to fight her own body," she says.

She went for a thirty-mile run in the Santa Monica Mountains around her home. The run reminded her of what her body was capable of: The years of long and intensive runs, hikes, and bike rides had taught her she could meet both physical and mental challenges head-on. There was no reason why this should be any different, she thought. There was no reason cancer should stop her.

That night, when her friend, photographer Tony DiZinno, came over to comfort her, she greeted him at the door with a big smile. "I bring chocolate and wine, love and comfort," he said, holding up the goods in each hand. That's when she knew it was going to be okay. She would continue to have doubts that would haunt her, but just like when running a marathon or an ultra, she would push those thoughts away and focus on the moment.

□ □ □

Growing up in South Africa, Louise was always athletic, and her father was a huge rugby fan. She would go to every game with him and knew all of the ins and outs of the teams. When she moved to California in the early '80s, when she was in her twenties, she noticed right away that people were a lot less physical in America than in South Africa. She thought about signing up for a gym until she noticed that the women there seemed to be more interested in matching their legwarmers to their leotards than getting fit. So instead, she bought a pair of running shoes and started exploring the roads and trails surrounding Los Angeles. She instantly fell in love with how strong running made her feel.

In 1983, a friend of hers suggested she do something called the Lawyer's Run, which went the length of Mulholland Drive, from Hollywood to Leo Carillo State Beach—a total of fifty-four miles. She went ahead and signed up but didn't realize until she was actually running the race that many of the other competitors were running as relay teams, taking about ten miles each. "I kept passing teams along the way, thinking, *How come I am doing this solo?*" Louise says. But she charged on through the windy curves and spectacular views of the San Fernando Valley, eventually running downhill toward the infinite blue of the Pacific Ocean. Afterward, the friend who suggested she sign up for it said, "I didn't really think you would *do* it." It turned out he was just joking.

But what started as a joke became a serious running career. Now fifty-three, Louise has run seven Hawaii Ironmans. She has raced with teams in three Raid Gauloises, which is widely considered to be one of the most difficult and prestigious multisport adventure races there is. She has done more than sixty marathons and a dozen ultra runs, including a second-place finish at the infamous Badwater, a 135-mile race through Death Valley in the 120-degree heat of July.

When Louise first started competing seriously, she was in her thirties and married. She and her husband did everything together from the hundred-mile ultras to adventure racing. Their marriage lasted for fifteen years, ending not long before she got cancer. When they split up, she began doing things on her own. She found it was refreshing and empowering. With her husband around, she had someone to push her, but often she found that wasn't the kind of push she needed. She was competitive—but ultimately only against herself.

After Louise was diagnosed with breast cancer, she found herself competing alone in the purest sense, mind against body. Louise went through two more surgeries in the span of a few months in an attempt to eradicate the cancer. First, thirty-three lymph nodes were removed. Then her doctors took out more tissue and gave her a partial mastectomy to make sure all of the traces of cancer were gone.

After each surgery, she was left with stitches and a warning not to run for at least a week. But by day three after the second surgery, she figured out that in spite of the drain under her arm, she could still use the StairMaster. The fact that a nurse came by her house to change her dressings every day meant she had to time her workouts precisely if she didn't want to get caught. If a nurse was scheduled to arrive at 4:00 PM, she would jump on the StairMaster at 2:30 PM and hop off an hour later, take a shower, and appear as if she had done nothing physical at all. "I figured that the StairMaster isn't as jarring as pavement," Louise says. "So why not? By the end, I was so good at protecting my chest that I did manage to get back out on the trails to do some hiking before the drain came out." After the third and final surgery, she waited two days before she started running again, using her hands, once again, to stabilize her breast.

This might appear to be obsessive behavior to some, and Louise agrees that in retrospect, it seems that way even to her. But at the time, what it meant was that she was in control of her life. "Things just seemed to be tumbling out of control. Being able to exercise or get out every day and make those decisions gave me a sense of normalcy in a horribly abnormal situation."

Besides, the surgeries weren't what hit Louise the hardest. It was the drugs to follow. Because her oncologist was a close, personal friend and knew what her body was capable of, he suggested a higher-than-usual dose of chemotherapy. He wanted to use it to eradicate any possibility of the disease returning. "I wasn't aware at the time that they were giving me an increased dosage of the chemo drugs," says Louise. "I only found out afterward. It was a decision my doctor had made. Later adding another drug, called Herceptin, really cleared the margins." Herceptin was going through a trial in which doctors were trying to prove its efficiency in preventing the cancer from reoccurring. The drug had a success rate of 52 percent in helping prevent recurring cancer when combined with chemo, which was better than anything on the market at the time.

"My doctor's colleagues were saying that he was going to kill me with the dose of chemo he put me on," Louise says. "He said, 'I know her body. I know how much she can take.' He would check in with me and find out how far I ran every day to help raise and lower the doses. If I said I ran eight miles, he would up it, and if I told him I felt like an old man, we went down."

Louise was able to withstand the effects of the drugs, but they wiped out her endurance. "Chemo was doing its thing the way it did with anyone. The effects were cumulative. Your body gets slower and slower every treatment. It got to the point where I couldn't even go to the gym to lift weights because I had no strength."

Louise's friend, Tony DiZinno, knew that in order to keep Louise's spirits high, he needed to help her find something to focus on other than the cancer. He called an old buddy in New York, a TV producer who became interested in Louise's story. "I knew we didn't have time to throw a pity party or get morbid by thinking about the 'what ifs,'" he says. About two months into the chemo, CBS's *48 Hours* began filming her life—her cancer treatments, her runs, her job (she's an elementary school teacher at a private school in the San Fernando Valley), and the time she spent playing with her four dogs. Louise found herself in the middle of a media frenzy for almost a year and barely had time to think about the future.

Many might feel overwhelmed by this attention at such a difficult time, but Louise only saw the bright side. "It kept me focused on what was going on," she remembers, "but it also made me more aware of the details of the treatment. It made me more informed and kept me grounded. There was never this false sense of security. I knew how serious it was."

Tony continued to be one of Louise's biggest cheerleaders throughout her illness. When he went to the Raid Gauloises adventure race in Ecuador, which Louise and Tony had planned to go to together, he dyed his hair blond like hers to show his support of her, and when she went bald from the chemotherapy, he shaved his head.

A funny thing happened for Louise after her chemo was complete in the spring of 1999. For the first time, everyone who thought she was crazy for doing all of the endurance stuff she did (doctors, parents, etc.) now supported her to get back out there.

"My mother, who had always been so nervous about my races, was so excited that I was healthy again that all of the sudden she was encouraging me."

Throughout this time, Louise took refuge in her willpower to get out and regularly go running—or, when things were really bad, walking. There was a point when all she could do was walk a few blocks, but still, this was better than nothing. She had a number of friends who would go out with her every day, whether she could run ten miles or only a few blocks. Then, in February 1999, her friend Lisa Batchem-Smith called and talked her into doing the Badwater in July. Louise had never done the 135-mile race through the desert, but Lisa had won it in 1998 and thought the infamous competition was just the distraction Louise needed to complete her recovery.

Louise agreed. "I thought the timing was perfect," she says. "Others might have thought it was too soon. I was looking for something to focus on other than the cancer. I'm very goal-oriented, so I thought I might as well do something that is really challenging."

So it was time to prepare and time to train. She had a rough start, but she just kept at it. "I felt like I didn't know how to run," says Louise. "But eventually I would get back to running a mile without stopping, and then two, and then three. It was the small successes that kept me pushing on." In March 1999, Louise tested her strength and endurance with the Catalina Marathon. She found it excruciating to finish. "It's a difficult race because you start at the water, and everything goes up," she says. "At the finish, you come down again to the water. It's a very hilly, scenic race. I could barely run it. I had to keep reminding myself that I had just finished chemo and it wasn't me. It was the drugs."

Louise trained as hard as she ever had for this race in spite of being weak, and for a moment in late May, she thought the

Badwater was out of the question. One weekend she went to Death Valley with her support crew to do a training run. The plan was to run forty-three miles through one of the more difficult sections in the middle of the desert. At around mile 40, she stopped to rest for a minute, and her nose started to bleed. So she lay down. That was when her muscles started convulsing. Everything from her cheeks to her toes was going into spasms, and her team didn't know what to do. Finally, someone called 911. She was rushed to a nearby hospital and then airlifted to Las Vegas. The medics insisted she was dehydrated, but she knew otherwise. "I kept telling them, 'I am not dehydrated. I have been drinking enough water. It's something else.' And they kept pumping IVs into my arm," Louise remembers.

What the doctors in Las Vegas didn't know is that she had been on a low-sodium diet because she felt so bloated from the steroids she was taking for her cancer the previous months. By the next morning, the doctors finally determined that she had suffered from hypernatremia, a serious sodium deficiency. In an attempt to stop retaining so much water, she had cut back severely on her salt intake, buying no-salt tuna and no-salt crackers. "That's when I really started learning about the importance of nutrition," says Louise. "What is amazing is that in a race like the Badwater, if you are really committed, it's usually your body that will give up before your mind. So you have to really take care of your body so that your mind can stay focused on keeping you moving forward. It's an amazing sense of accomplishment when you know your body wants to quit and your mind pulls you through."

And Louise kept moving forward. Two months after Louise was airlifted out of Death Valley, she was standing at the start line for the Badwater. The gun went off, and for the rest of the day, it was one foot in front of the other as she followed the white line down a blistering hot highway, through the desolate landscape of Death

Valley. The starkness of it made her feel incredibly alive, and the waves of heat floating across the desert, blurring her vision, will forever be etched in her mind.

As the day wore on and the evening set in, a friend from Los Angeles, Tommy Baynard, was pacing Louise, who was by now exhausted. He noticed she wasn't running in a straight line but instead was weaving her way around on the blacktop. When he asked her what she was doing, she said very matter-of-factly, "Going around the old people in the chairs. I don't want to knock into them." When Tommy told her support crew this story later, they were amused but not surprised. The hallucinations Louise was experiencing were not a side effect of the drugs but of ultra running itself. Extreme fatigue and lack of sleep bring them on. "Hallucinations are so common in endurance activities that we don't really think about it. It's not like sleepwalking. It's more like you see things that are figments of your imagination. And they can be quite humorous," says Louise. "I've climbed over a fictitious barbecue, chased after men who weren't there on a hillside, I've even attempted to purchase a hat for a teammate from a ghost in the middle of the jungle. When the hallucinations start, there's just no stopping them until they play out. I have old teammates who I still laugh about old hallucinations when I see them. Group hallucinations, where you convince someone else that you are seeing something and they see it. Now those are the best."

So why does Louise put her body through all of this?

"In the middle of the Badwater, if you were to ask me why I do it, I would have no idea. That race is pure hell. I always tell my friends, 'If I talk about doing it again, remind me how awful it really is.' But then when it's over, the feeling is accomplishment. It's about passion, and I have that passion for running. I truly believe you have to pursue your passion, and it doesn't matter what your age is or how monumental the challenge is in front of you. If you don't have dreams, if you don't have something to pursue, how do you get up every day?"

Louise was the second woman to finish and was ninth overall. She credits her Badwater support team for inspiring her and leading her to the finish. She's learned over the last few years that without a solid support team around you, it's hard to be successful, whether running the Badwater or battling cancer.

"My life is interesting, my life is adventuresome, and sometimes it's just hard to find people who live on the edge like you do. So when I find those people, I try to hold onto them and surround myself with that kind of enthusiasm."

The perfect example of this was a race she ran last summer, a 250-mile stage race through the Sahara Desert that ended at the Sphinx, called Racing the Planet. It's a four-part race over seven days, part of a series of races that she plans on doing again. It will take her to various deserts from the Sahara to the frozen tundra of Antarctica. The race gets so hot and intense at times, water bottles explode from the heat. Though Louise says she thrives in the heat, she's nervous about what the cold will be like. But if she's learned anything over the years from her racing and her experience with cancer, this is the kind of long, lonely race where companionship is important. After her races are over, Louise always makes a point of racing with friends and supporting those around her in a race.

"It's nice just to have somebody next to you, that companionship when you are out there in the empty desert. I don't necessarily want conversation. When I go by somebody, I'll always say, 'Hi, how you feeling? You look strong, do you need water? It's hotter than bloody hell right now.' I'll make some comment. Just like life—we're all in this together."

Nowadays, Louise typically runs fourteen to sixteen hours per week. Some days she does a quick five miles, while on others, she'll do thirty. She also cross-trains, bikes, paddles, and lifts weights. But running is still her main sport. And friends are still her main support. "I have different friends who will run with me," she says. "Sometimes one friend will meet me for half of the run, and then another will meet me for the second half. I even have one friend who lives thirty miles away. I run to her house and she makes me breakfast, then drives me home. I like her a lot," she says, laughing.

Seven years after her diagnosis, she is still free of cancer. "But you always have that fear it could come back," Louise admits. "It's not a constant, conscious fear, but it's always there every time you go for a checkup, every time there's something unusual with your body. Like if you have a bad headache, it's like, *Oh my God, do I have brain cancer?* I don't obsess over it, and I don't think about it daily, but it's something that niggles there all the time. I am conscious of it because there are no guarantees."

In 2006, Louise turned fifty-three, and although her race times have slowed a bit, she herself hasn't. But with age she's become less concerned with speed. "Your priorities change as you get older," she says. "Now my focus is finishing. This is not to say I am not competitive. If I see someone up ahead of me, I definitely think, *If I only go a little faster, I can take them.* Then I go for it. But now it's not about winning. It's about completing monumental hurdles."

Chapter Thirteen: Renaissance Runner

It's rare to find someone who's equally passionate about a number of outdoor sports and even more rare that this person is top-ranked in all of them. But runner, rock climber, and backcountry and Nordic skier Jeannie Wall is just that: an avid outdoorswoman and accomplished athlete who has captured the attention of those in the sports world with her amazing feats and thirst for the ultimate challenge.

Jeannie, who is thirty-eight, doesn't consider herself to be a professional runner even though she's taken part in numerous grueling trail runs. She wouldn't even necessarily call herself a professional athlete, yet she's well-known in the outdoors world for a variety of sports. In addition to being a runner, Jeannie is an avid rock climber and a nationally ranked Nordic skier who just missed the cut for the Olympic team in 1994 and in 2002. She won the Great American Birkebeiner in 2002, one of the most prestigious cross-country marathon races. She regularly completes challenges like the Bighorn 50K and the Bridger Ridge Race, and the Rim to Rim "fun" run around the Grand Canyon.

These days, though, she'd rather go out for a thirty-mile run with friends over racing. In spite of her accomplishments, Jeannie doesn't consider herself a professional athlete because she does it all for the love of the outdoors. For her, going out into the woods for an all-day run or an intense backcountry ski doesn't mean she's an "endurance freak"—as she's been called—that's just how she enjoys life. In 2004, she was featured in an *Outside* magazine article in which she was called "the Energizer Bunny," and she's never lived that title down. In her defense, she told *Skiing* magazine a year later, "I'm not some junkie who needs my fix every day." She just loves to be out in the wild. This in turn has led to a successful career as a product-line developer for the outdoor-clothing company Patagonia.

□ □ □

If ever there was a woman who understands survival of the fittest, it's Jeannie. She grew up in Madison, Wisconsin, as the youngest of eleven children, and was always scrapping for whatever was left over, from athletic gear to lunch money. "By the time *I* came around, my parents were so tired that they pretty much let me do whatever I wanted. Being athletic and being outside kind of gave me sanity and some direction not easily found in the chaos of a large family," she says.

She spent her childhood riding her bike and running through the neighborhood freely, exploring as she went. She now attributes this freedom to her self-confidence. "I always thought I could do whatever I wanted—I think because my parents never said no. Later, I realized not every girl is as fortunate. I definitely looked at people doing cool things when I was growing up, like climbing a mountain or swimming across the English Channel, and thought, *I am going to do whatever I want when I grow up.*"

Jeannie's love of running started with her older sister Anne, who ran triathlons and marathons. She used to let Jeannie run with her and her friends, never treating her like a kid sister who was just in the way. "I didn't really start running until about ninth grade, but when I did, I just kind of got hooked. I started running every day after school. The more I ran, the more I realized I was done with team competition. It was too narrow for me, mentally and physically," Jeannie says. She says this was a key point in her life, because it helped her learn to make decisions and listen to her instincts. "Later on, in life and in my career, I would go down a path that was more about following my heart than doing what I was expected to do. Running seemed to give me the initial strength for that."

By age twenty, Jeannie started running more seriously, completing her first marathon in 1988, during her sophomore year of college. A friend convinced her to sign up for the Chicago Marathon with him, saying that if she could do a two-hour run with him, she was ready for the marathon. With only three weeks of training and a couple of long runs under her belt, she drove to Chicago. She had no idea how to pace herself and by mile 20 was suffering from severe stomach cramps. Still, she managed to complete the marathon in 3:23—only a few minutes away from making the cut for automatic entry into the Boston Marathon. "It was a turning point for me, changing my thinking about what I could do athletically," says Jeannie. "I realized then that the perceptions I had were just perceptions, and I had to start breaking them down, to just go after things in life."

Jeannie started reorganizing her priorities and decided to change her major from business—the "fallback major" in her family—to journalism. Upon graduation, she wrote to Patagonia, telling them she wanted to work for them and offering to fly herself to their headquarters in California for an interview. They ended up hiring her, thus sending her down a new path in life.

Jeannie came to Patagonia with plenty of fresh ideas. For one, she had been annoyed with the increase in technical enhancements she was seeing on clothing. She thought there were too many zippers, pockets, and unnecessary toggles, and she felt strongly that apparel for trail running needed to be hassle-free. "It also needs to breathe well and dry quickly but be able to go through any kind of weather," she says. "I think this helps make running purer, simpler. Simplicity is already an important element in running, so the clothing should mimic that. There is a flip side to technology, and I think unfortunately too many people get caught up in it and take too much junk out with them when they go for a run. When I head out, I go with as little as possible, because I feel freer, and that's what I love about running. It's not gear intensive."

In the early '90s, Jeannie came up with the idea for the Endurance line, a handful of products to support people who weren't just interested in going rock climbing and mountaineering, but engaging in many different outdoor activities, especially running. The line needed to be flexible, comfortable, and breathable—but most importantly, light. "At the time, I was a runner, a Nordic skier, and a cyclist, and there wasn't much for athletes like me." So she pitched her idea for this kind of gear to Patagonia, backed up by a lot of research and a detailed business plan, and they thought it was a marketable idea.

Jeannie's decision to encourage Patagonia to design the Endurance line wasn't just gear-based. She says that a respect for the outdoors and sustainability—a less-is-more approach—has influenced her on the job and in the backcountry. "I believe small is beautiful, and ultimately, as good as it is to give back, the simpler we live, the more we pay attention and have compassion for all living things, the better off our world will be," she says.

□ □ □

Trail running is simple. This is a big part of the reason Jeannie loves it. It started to become a passion for her when she made the move from Madison, Wisconsin, to Ventura, California, the home of Patagonia, at the age of twenty-four. The Los Padres National Forest surrounding Ventura offer endless trails into some seriously remote terrain. She had a friend who regularly took her out into these mountains. He had completed the Western States Endurance Run the previous year, so he convinced her to run an ultra—the Angeles Crest 50—with him.

At the time, she thought he was crazy because she had never run more than a marathon. "That race was, again, about changing my whole mindset," she remembers. "I think this is important, especially for women—we easily let ourselves get boxed into what we can and can't do." Her first ultra race went well, and she was in second place for most of the course. Then, in the last ten miles, she started to get tired and slipped back. But that was okay with her. "When I got toward the end, it occurred to me that this was the longest run I had ever done, and that I had no idea I could do it."

While racing has been an on-again, off-again interest for Jeannie, her love of running has stayed constant. "All of these breakthroughs I kept having came through running more than other sports because it is such a pure form of a sport," she says. "There's not a lot of technical stuff or money involved. You can do it all over the world, so it really gives you this huge sense of freedom."

One of the most memorable—and challenging—endurance races Jeannie has ever done was a forty-two-mile rim to rim to rim of the Grand Canyon, ten years ago. "We started at five in the morning. It was cold—not just a spring chill, but full winter cold," she says. She and a small group of friends stood at the top of the Grand Canyon, looking out into the darkness with their headlamps, and then were off. They would gain 10,000 feet in elevation over the course of twelve hours; they would experience every type of weather situation, including snow; and they would battle both their bodies and their minds, forging on until the entire distance was completed. Jeannie has never forgotten that run for the colors, the climate changes, the friendships, the silence, and that meditative, simplified state of bliss.

"I ran it a few years later with some friends," she recalls, "but the first time is what stands out in my mind. It was one of those moments where I look back, and it was hard, but it was so beautiful. The ebb and flow of our group was amazing, and there were some not-so-easy times we had to work through."

For a while, living in Ventura was a good change for Jeannie. And it was definitely good for her running, thanks to the year-round mild temperature. But after more than three years without winter, she was anxious for the snow, and she ended up moving to Patagonia's office in Bozeman, Montana. It was in Bozeman that she finally was able to sink herself into winter sports, something she'd wanted to do since she was a kid but wasn't able to because of her large family. "I wanted to be an alpine skier as a kid, but my dad's response was, 'There's no way I'm driving you across town. I have other kids to take care of,'" she remembers.

At age twenty-six, she picked up Nordic skiing and quickly excelled at it, making it to the Olympic trials by her fifth race, in 1994. She narrowly missed a spot on the team. Montana was also where Jeannie was able to begin what she calls her "winter running": randonee skiing. Also called "ski mountaineering" or "alpine touring," randonee is a form of backcountry skiing that mixes the free-heeled motion for climbing with the alpine skiing technique for descent. The difference between telemark gear and randonee gear is especially apparent in the binding because in randonee, the binding allows the heel to lock down in descent as opposed the free heel of telemark skiing.

Randonee requires stamina for uphill and long distances, and mountaineering techniques for glacier traverses. "'Randonée' is the French word for 'walking,' but for me," says Jeannie, "it's a very similar motion to running, especially when I am just touring in the backcountry. It has opened up a whole world to me. It takes me to all of those wild and beautiful places that I couldn't get to otherwise in the winter, and it gives me that connectedness to nature that I get when I run trails."

Jeannie first got serious about it 1996, when two friends convinced her to join them in a randonee race in Sweden, where they dug a snow cave and slept out overnight midrace. The sense of adventure, the speed, and the challenge all resonated with her. While Jeannie has competed in a number of trail running races around the world, she has found that over the years, she has lost her passion for competing in trail running, preferring to just go into the backcountry with her friends for a long afternoon run. With randonee, her fire for competition was rekindled briefly. In 2002, after eight years as a Nordic skier, she started competing in the women's randonee circuit, dominating the sport. She won the American Ski Mountaineering Championships three times, and also won the Wasatch Powderkeg, a race that travels up and down a mountain, covering fourteen miles between Alta and Brighton resorts in Utah. She also placed fifth at the World Championships race in Europe, competing against racers who train year-round.

Jeannie has been racing in one way or another for much of her life, yet she has a healthy attitude about winning and losing. "I've learned that competition doesn't have to make you feel inadequate," she says. "The world is a competitive place, but I also think it's really important to know how to turn competitiveness on

and off, and to understand when it's appropriate. I think it would
be healthy for girls to grow up competing more and learning how
this can be good for them. Competition in sports can be used to
a woman's advantage later in life if she is not afraid of somebody
trying to compete with her."

□ □ □

Running a 100K with a friend brought this home for her. The friend
asked Jeannie not to compete with her but to run alongside her for
the duration of the race. It was tough for Jeannie. Midway through,
she felt herself struggling with the desire to push harder because
she knew she could, but she knew she had promised her friend she
would stay with her. "I remember when she first asked me to run
the race with her, she said, 'I need you to run it with me, not ahead
of me.' I remember thinking to myself, *Well, then, why are we doing
a race?"* Jeannie says. She ran with her friend until the last ten miles
of the race, when her friend told her to go ahead, that she was fine
on her own. It was then that Jeannie realized what an important
lesson her friend had taught her. "I learned two things that day.
How to not be competitive with my friends, and that the reason I
race is that it gives me the chance to be competitive in the realm of a
competitive event, not when I am just out enjoying an activity with
my friends. There was a noticeable difference for me after that day
when I went out for a run or a ski with friends."

On that day, Jeannie pushed hard the rest of the race and ended
up in third place, but it was unimportant. What had been most
important about the race was that she ran with her friend for most
of it and shared the experience with someone she cared about.

For Jeannie, being an athlete also means building a relationship with nature. "For me, getting into the backcountry, whether on foot or skis, is not about speed," says Jeannie. "It's about going into the wilderness and finding some kind of connection. Getting out there gives me a sense of awe and a spiritual feeling that I need in my life to get refueled. It's where I get my best thoughts and clarity on my life or work. It's where I enjoy the friendships, and I can push myself. Like with running, I can push myself far, and there's nothing really stopping me."

Because of running, Jeannie has learned to have faith in herself and her capabilities. "Running and racing has helped me know what my body can do and how hard I can push. When you have tested your body in those safe places, you learn where you can take yourself mentally when you are in a real situation. I find I don't get wigged out because I know just how deep I can dig."

Chapter Fourteen: Winning Isn't the Only Thing

Seemingly out of nowhere, thirty-two-year-old Lornah Kiplagat burst upon the international running scene when she crossed the finish line to win the Los Angeles Marathon in 1997. But actually,

she didn't come out of nowhere. She had been training very seriously and very hard on the Kenyan national team for the past two years, with specific goals in mind. She was determined to become a champion, but just not for the glory of it. She wanted the prize money too.

But don't get the wrong idea. Becoming a world-class distance runner wasn't a get-rich-quick scheme for Lornah. She had bigger plans. With the large amounts of money she could earn by winning big races, she could help the young Kenyan girls who would one day follow in her footsteps. She could make their lives easier than hers had been.

Life in Kenya is not easy for most people, but this is especially so for women, who are pretty much considered property, not very different from cattle. When Lornah got it into her head at twenty years old that she would become a runner, she was immediately faced with obstacles of all kinds: financial, practical, and most of all, social. Women all over the world experience disapproval from family for training in sports, but in Kenya, this is especially true. Parents—and, once daughters are married off, husbands—rarely let girls pursue running careers because it means one less person will be able to care for the children and work on the farm. Running is seen as a waste of time when a girl could be doing something for her family, like cooking or tending to children.

Since winning the Los Angeles Marathon, Lornah has gone to the Olympics and has raced around the world. She eventually moved to Holland and now runs with the Dutch team. But she hasn't left her homeland behind: In 2000, she founded a girls' race camp in Kenya, the High Altitude Training Center (HATC), in a town called Iten. Every year, she spends four months training there and donates $50,000 of her winnings to it, and it has become Kenya's premier training spot for young women. As of 2006, twelve women who have been through the camp are contenders for the 2008 Olympics. Lornah is very proud of this, even if it means these girls are competing for a spot she herself could be filling. It's this kind of confidence—matched with compassion for other Kenyan women—that makes her a role model. "Every second of my path has been motivation for me," says Lornah, "because I don't want any other girl to have the kind of experience I did," she says of her isolated and challenging beginning as a runner.

Lornah was born in the southeastern part of Kenya, into a tribe called the Kalenjin. She grew up on a *shamba*—the Swahili word for farm—on three-hundred acres high above the Great Rift Valley in the mountains in the western part of Kenya. Most of the Kalenjin living in this region live eight-thousand feet or more above sea level.

The landscape has been described as rolling hills of red earth, dotted with scraggly trees. The temperature is about eighty degrees year-round, great for running. The rains come short and hard, then leave again, and the earth dries quickly, sucking the water deep into the cracked soil.

It's no secret that Kenya has a reputation for producing a number of truly incredible runners. Of those who have become well-known, many are Kalenjin. *Outside* magazine writer Christopher McDougall reported in September 2000 that the Kalenjin's running secret is not just their high altitude and warm climate, but their lifestyle, which "mandates a combination of huge mileage, relentless race-caliber intensity, and an every-man-for-himself attitude."

World-renowned Kalenjin runners include Tegla Lorupe, the female world record holder for the 20,000- and 25,000-meter races, and, of course, Kipchoge Keino, who (along with other Kenyan gold medal runners Naftali Temu for the 1,000 meter and Amos Biwott in the 3,000-meter steeplechase) took the 1968 Mexico City Olympics by storm. Keino's story is unforgettable and exemplifies the Kenyan spirit. He arrived in Mexico City not knowing he had a gallbladder infection and was told he was too ill to compete. At the last minute, however, he decided he couldn't let his country down. He jumped into a taxi and headed to the Olympic stadium. But traffic was awful, so he got out of the cab and ran the few remaining miles to the stadium. He then proceeded to win the 1,500-meter race by 20 meters—a record victory in that event to this day.

The Kenyan dominance in the Olympics that year paved the way for the country's running reputation. Ever since, young Kenyans have grown up knowing that they could be Olympians. Susan Sirma, Lornah's cousin, grew up knowing this, and she ended up becoming the first woman to win an Olympic medal for Kenya, when she got the bronze in the 1,500-meter race in 1988.

Lornah herself was planning to follow the path her parents wanted for her—to become a doctor. But when she saw what was possible with Susan, she knew she too had to give it a try. She too would become a runner. But first, she would have to overcome many difficult obstacles.

□ □ □

"My family didn't support me at first. They wanted me to study," says Lornah. "Only when I became really good did they accept it. For women it was very hard to find training facilities, and it was a tough time for me." But when Susan heard about Lornah's dream, she took her in, helped her find a place to live and work, and most importantly, ran alongside her daily. "Susan remains my heroine to date," says Lornah. "She really helped me become what I am today." At first, however, Susan had her doubts, because Lornah seemed a little heavy to be a runner. But within a few months, she realized she was wrong.

In 1995, at the age of twenty, Lornah could run as fast as Susan, who was then considered to be one of the fastest women in the world. Now she was ready for the next step. She got on a bus and traveled two hundred miles to Nairobi to try out for the national team. Because she knew no one in the capital city, she slept in a public bathroom near the tryout location. After a sleepless night curled up in the bathroom, she emerged and lined up to race. She hadn't had breakfast, but that was the last thing on her mind.

It was a cross-country race, and there were a hundred other women. Only six would be chosen for the team. The gun went off, and Lornah ran—hard. She placed sixth, earning her a place on the national team and putting her on the road to becoming a world-class runner.

After running successfully in her own country for a year—a place full of championship runners—she went international with the Kenyan team. In 1997, she made her debut and established herself as a force to be reckoned with internationally by winning the Los Angeles Marathon in 2:33:50. She repeated the Los Angeles Marathon win in 1998 with a time of 2:33:58. In 2000 she set a personal record, placing second in a Lisbon half marathon with a time of 1:06:56. Her achievements continued when she broke the world record for a 20K with a time of 1:03:54 in 2001.

That 20K was a memorable and challenging race for Lornah. It took place on a cold day in March in the Netherlands. It was windy, and the course was a completely flat loop in the middle of an open field. The wind was problematic for many of the runners, but somehow, Lornah knew she would be fast that day, and she knew she wanted a world record. "This race was tough for me because I knew that with the wind, I had to give it all, that I had to overcome it. I was fighting more than other runners—I was fighting nature."

After establishing her world-class status as a road runner, she decided in 2003 to become a track runner—a transition rarely made in the running world. "Switching to track was a great challenge. I liked the ten-K on the road, so I thought, *Why not compete in the ten-thousand on track?* It's the same distance, just another surface and atmosphere," she says.

She didn't run for her native Kenya though, instead opting to compete for her new home, the Netherlands. "They were very supportive of my running, and I lived there, so I didn't feel like I was abandoning my country. I just was running for my new home," she explains.

In 2005, Lornah won the 6,500-meter race at the European Cross Country Championship, finishing with an impressive time of 19:55. "This was a really special race for me," she says, "because it was the first time Holland hosted this event, and having a win like this—it could not be better." Lornah will spend her winter training in Kenya, and most of 2006 will be focused on getting ready for the 2008 Beijing Olympic trials. Her switch to track was surprising, but her Dutch husband, Pieter, knows to expect the unexpected from Lornah. "She was always really different," Pieter says of his wife. "That's the reason I really liked her. If something is in her mind, my God, nothing can stop her."

□ □ □

By now, Lornah has grown accustomed to people questioning her unorthodox choices, and she takes it in stride. When she first started organizing the girls' training camp, she caught some flak. "Many people said to me, 'Why are you putting money into this? Why not build a dispensary?' And that would be nice to do, but that is something else. The girls are good athletes, and they should have this. Even if a girl does not make it as a runner—not all of them have talent for running—they learn skills at camp and can go back to their communities and start their own businesses. This is what we hope for."

When she won her first chunk of money, it went toward building a camp where women were treated the same as men. While training in Kenya, she had won a number of international races in relatively quick succession and had gained some recognition, yet she still found herself, along with the women on other teams, washing the laundry and shoes of the men runners. "We trained a lot in the mud, and I was training as hard as them and then cleaning their socks and shoes. I decided I wouldn't do it anymore. At some camps, this is still happening, but not in my camp."

The HATC is free of charge for women, but men must pay. And if any man comes to the camp with an expectation of women cleaning up after him, he is quickly shown the door. The center sits atop a beautiful green hillside at eight-thousand feet. It's a fantastic place to train (Lornah herself trains here four months a year) because the temperature never falls below seventy degrees, it rarely rains, and there are twelve hours of daylight year-round. To keep costs down, the camp is simple, consisting of no more than a smattering of buildings on a few acres. They also just opened a gym, so the athletes can add weights to their workout schedule.

Twice a year, the camp holds a race in Kenya with an open invitation to any girl who wants to try for a camp scholarship. Lornah takes on five new girls a year from this race, taking them away from the farms where they work constantly and allowing them to focus on running and running only for a few weeks or even a few months. The rest of the year, Lornah requires that the girls go to boarding school if they want to keep training with the camp. Even though these are publicly funded, girls must pay for essentials such as books, which often means they are cost-prohibitive. If a girl is accepted into Lornah's program, boarding school fees are paid for.

Even if the camp doesn't turn the girl into a world-class runner, she learns other skills, like cooking and computers, in the hope that she can apply them—along with her newfound confidence—to working in her community. "We hope that when they go home with their new knowledge, that this change in them helps change their small communities. A few of the girls have gone home and opened businesses in their towns," Lornah says.

Unlike many camps that have title sponsors, like Nike or Saucony, Lornah herself pays to keep the operation running. Her girls stay at the camp for free, but she is able to offset some expenses by taking a $20 a day lodging fee from other runners who are interested in training. These are usually Westerners, recreational and competitive runners who want to find what makes Kenyans such powerful runners. Still, even with Western visits, the cost of running the camp and sponsoring the girls ends up being about $50,000 a year—an amount she feels overwhelmed by at times. "We hope someday the camp will pay for itself, but as long as I keep winning, I can pay for it," Lornah says. She dreams about making the camp self-sufficient with solar power and planting a garden so fresh vegetables are readily available. But all of this takes time and money, and the camp is still young.

Lornah knows that dreams are important, but so is reality. This is why she requires that every girl accepted to HATC must also keep up with her studies, and other nearby camps are seeing the value of this and have started adopting the rule. "It used to be that a young person would be pulled out of school to go to camp and learn to run," Lornah says. "Then if they were injured or their career was over quickly, they had nothing when they finished, and no education."

In many cases, Lornah and Pieter pay as much as $400 per year for a girl who came from a farm to continue her education at a government-run boarding school. Why doesn't she open a school on the camp's grounds? "You can't just do that in Kenya. The schools are government-run, and to open a school would be difficult," Lornah explains. "We don't have the books, the desks, everything it takes. It's easier for us now to send them to school. We could really use help paying for this because it's one of our biggest expenses right now."

In 2002, sportswriter Lori Shontz spent a few weeks at the camp, writing a series of articles about Kenyan women runners. "I was amazed at how busy everyone was all the time," she remembers. "There was one day when I was interviewing the girls where I had to wash dishes with them for three hours in order to get the interview. I kept telling them I had to go to the bathroom and running back to my room to take notes because they were too shy for me to record them. They must have thought I went to the bathroom a lot." Lori says one of the things that she was most impressed with was how dedicated the girls were to the camp and to Lornah.

Lori continues to explain that twice a day, at 6:00 AM and 4:00 PM, the girls—and the rest of the town—would take a break from their work for organized exercise, turning Iten into a town of runners. Anyone seen running outside of these times was usually a *muguzu* (white person). "There was definitely a rigid schedule there. When three-thirty would roll around, if the exercise field was full of animals, they would be cleared so that the four o'clock workout wouldn't be held up," she remembers.

Lori was also struck by Lornah's attitude about handouts: Whether money or just gifts, she had a strict policy that visitors were not to give things to the girls. Because of her own life experience, she knows it is a bad idea to create any expectation that things in life are given for nothing. Lornah thinks getting handouts leads to laziness, and as Ethiopians and Moroccans have started to gain on Kenyans in the running ranks, she is especially vigilant against any slacking. In her opinion, if the Kenyan women have it too easy, they won't be as hungry to win, to work for things, and to make the right choices in life.

Lori experienced this sentiment firsthand one day. She had lost her room key while on a run, and later in the day, a girl found and returned it to her. Lori wanted to give her a reward, but Lornah wouldn't allow it, pointing out that the girl shouldn't get money for an act she should be doing anyway.

For Lornah, "handouts" were offered as soon as she won her first major international competition, the Los Angeles Marathon, in 1997. Even though people thought she was crazy, she turned them down first, saying that she wasn't ready to be considered the best—yet. When she was ready, she would begin taking sponsors. One of the first ones she took was Saucony. She became acquainted with the marketing director, Pieter Langerhost, who would send her shoes and socks. Every time he sent something, Lornah would send a thank-you note, which surprised him and made him want to know more about this young Kenyan woman. Eventually, her relationship with Pieter became more than a friendship, and he quit his job at Saucony to become her agent. And in spite of being sixteen years older than her, he became her husband as well. Together, they began to build her dreams: to become one of the best women runners in the world, and to start the training camp.

"We have made a lot of change in the Kenyan society in five years," Lornah says. "I am very proud of this. We teach the girls to do things. We keep them in school and don't let them drop out. This has changed the mindset across the country, and we see girls realizing they need to share work opportunities at home—and to tell boyfriends and husbands that they need to help too. Runners who come from our camp can go back into the community and help improve living standards for all Kenyans."

Chapter Fifteen: Unpacking the "Girl Box"

"**W**hat is keeping me from leaving the hotel room?" Shari Kunz asked herself. It was January 2003, and she was in Charlotte, North Carolina, thousands of miles from her home and family in Hailey, Idaho. She had recently become a council director for Girls on the Run—a nonprofit youth program aimed at helping young girls find self-confidence through running—and had come to North Carolina to attend a conference for the organization.

She was supposed to be a mentor to these girls, yet here she was, having a minor panic attack in a hotel room far from home. She had no idea what she was doing there: She had no confidence, she felt out of place, and she just knew she didn't have the skills she needed to do this. She didn't even know what a "nonprofit" was when she took this on. Now, suddenly, she was an accidental leader, and there was no turning back. "As I sat in that hotel room, I realized I was at a crossroads in my life, with the opportunity to bring a miracle into little girls' lives. I realized I couldn't look back. I was physically being pushed out of my safety zone, and it was running that was doing this."

□ □ □

Shari ran her first marathon in Portland, Oregon, in October 2001. After that, running became her new passion. The marathon was for the Leukemia and Lymphoma Society, and she did it for her brother Paul, who was battling cancer. "I saw an ad for the run one day, and it wasn't like, *Oh, that's nice.* It was more like, *I have to do that.* At the time I was still in denial about Paul's illness. We all were. I was grasping at anything that seemed like it could help him."

Prior to the marathon, Shari had never seriously run, nor had she ever trained for anything. But now she trained every day, and even after the marathon was over, she managed to continue running through the winter, spring, and summer. Each day she would put on her shoes and head out the door, first running on the bike paths around her home and then eventually working up toward mountain trails.

Training for the marathon was the first time Shari can remember ever committing to something so wholeheartedly. Prior to her training, she had thought of herself as the type of person who never really finished anything. "I was a quitter when I was a kid. I remember wanting to get a clarinet. My parents said, 'No, you'll just quit. You quit everything.' I just remember those words, 'You quit everything.' So I grew up quitting everything. It was a self-fulfilling prophecy. Then I started training for my first marathon, and I didn't quit that. That was the first step for me. Then I ran my first marathon. I didn't quit that either. I just remember crossing the finish line, and it was so cool. It changed my life."

On the day of the marathon, Paul was in remission—or so they thought. She ran, meditating throughout the miles, thanking God, her friends, her family, everyone she could think of, for helping her get to that moment in time. She put one foot in front of the other, eighteen miles, nineteen miles, and then, when she rounded a corner at mile 20, there was Paul, standing on the sidelines and cheering for her. "He was my beacon, my guiding light," Shari remembers. "He was fighting so hard, and I ran those last few miles for him." They hugged for a long time afterward. "My first finish line brought more than just a race. It bonded me to my family and to my brother," Shari says. And her confidence skyrocketed. "I learned I could do something big from beginning to end. I could train, stick with it, and actually run a marathon. Not once but three times," says Shari. Eight months later, she did the San Diego Rock 'n' Roll marathon with her sister. Twelve months after her first Portland Marathon, she ran her third marathon (Portland again), and this time with her husband, Kyle.

Unfortunately, Paul's cancer came back after Christmas of 2001, and he died by the next Thanksgiving.

□ □ □

Shari's interest in Girls on the Run started after a hike with her family. On the car ride home, she read an article about the program's founder, Molly Barker, in *Runners World*. At one point, she started to cry.

"Kyle, listen to this," she said, and started reading out loud. "'The girls learn to believe in themselves and stand up for what they know is right, regardless of what their peers think or expect,'" the article read *(Runners World,* July 2002).

"Imagine having the opportunity as a girl to build that kind of courage with something healthy like running. I wish I'd had something like that," she says. "Now, looking back on it, I am not sure why it touched me so much, because it was just a one-page article about this organization." Seeing her reaction to the piece, her husband encouraged her to call the organization. It took her a little while to get her courage up, but one day she did.

In 2003, at her first Girls on the Run conference, Shari started writing in a journal. She wanted to be able read it years later and remember what she felt after her brother's death and starting the program. One of the entries reads:

> *In a year, I will have written a grant and obtained money to bring this program to my girls. I will have a board of directors who will have a passion for this like I do, and they will believe in this program as I do. I will have two schools with two principals who are grateful for this program. I will have coaches whom I love and girls who will realize how lucky they are to have this program. And in spite of all of this, I will still be surprised and wonder, How did I get here? Is this really me?*

That first day in the hotel room, she thought she had made a mistake signing up for this. By the last day of the conference, it all began to make sense. She had spent most of her life just going through the motions—getting married, having kids, doing what she thought she was supposed to do. Running the marathon had been a huge step in doing something out of the norm. Participating in Girls on the Run was to be the next step in her personal growth.

Unlike Shari, Molly Barker, the program's founder, had been running since she was fifteen years old, and she loved it. It made her feel strong, beautiful, free, and confident. She noticed that when she would stop running, she would fall back into what she later named "the Girl Box"—the world of societal restraints, that mysterious feeling that stopped her and her friends from raising their hands in class after a certain age, the thing that made them focus more on their outward appearance instead of what was inside.

"I coined the term 'Girl Box' to describe the dark place that girls—previously happy, confident girls—reluctantly go into about the time of fifth grade, often with heartbreaking results," writes Molly in her book *Girls on Track*. "The girl who knew all the answers becomes the girl who hides in the back of the class; the girl who could beat the boys at races becomes the girl who feels ashamed of her strong body and legs; the girl who giggled with her friends becomes the girl who is silent and afraid. . . . Through my own experiences and those of others, I realized that in the Girl Box, women suddenly perform their lives, as opposed to experiencing them. Down in the darkness of the Girl Box, they lose their spirit and morph into whatever they believe society wants them to be: what they see in magazines; what they see on television; what they see in their own families. I know this all too well, as I too am a former inhabitant of the Girl Box."

Molly met Shari the second year she started the program. She was impressed with Shari's enthusiasm and how well the program worked with her personality. "Shari is one of those people whom you feel lucky to run across in life. She's completely committed to the girls, and she understands how important her work is—not just to her community, but also to herself. It's a rare person who can see and accept that their charity work is more than just the act of giving, but the act of learning about yourself too."

Molly and Shari agree that running is the perfect way to give girls the strength, courage, and ability to complete tasks and steer themselves forward from girl to young woman. And so far, it seems to be working.

In spring of 2003, Elizabeth Hamachek, a full-time ski coach for the Sun Valley youth development racing teams, "ran into" Girls on the Run while jogging one day on a bike path in Ketchum, Idaho. She saw some young girls running toward her, and she recognized them, as she had trained a number of them over the years. When she asked them what they were doing, they told her they were in the middle of a 5K race. Some of the girls were walking and some jogging, so Elizabeth encouraged them to get back into it by running with them. At the end of the race, Elizabeth met Shari.

"I was drawn to the program by the basic principles of healthy lifestyles for girls," says Elizabeth, who signed up on the spot that day as a volunteer coach for Girls on the Run. "And then there was Shari. From the get-go, she has been one of the most positive people I have ever met in my life. Every time she would show up, she would have so much enthusiasm that it was infectious."

In fall of 2002, when Shari started her branch of Girls on the Run, there were already over a hundred branch organizations around the country. Shari didn't really think about what starting the group would entail, she just dove in. As her brother got sicker, she looked at it as a tribute to him, and her activity distracted her from her grief. She wasn't afraid to show her sadness to the girls, but at the same time, she wanted to show them that something positive could come out of his illness.

There were fourteen girls in the first program, including her own daughter, who was then nine years old. They met twice a week, on Mondays and Wednesdays, after school. Shari was a new runner and new at being an organizer, so she relied on volunteers to help her get the program figured out. "It's amazing that it all worked out, because I was just like, 'Hello, I am going to take your daughters, and we are going to run around, and it's going to be really great for them.' I can't believe people trusted that I knew what I was doing."

The Girls on the Run headquarters in North Carolina provided the foundation for the group, which included interactive life lessons to go with the physical activities. They encouraged Shari to get the girls to keep journals and to come up with her own games. While they gave her a diving board to jump from, she had to provide the motivation and the spirit—so there was no way she would quit the program, despite her doubts. "This went against everything I thought I was," she says with a laugh. "I never saw myself running a nonprofit or doing all of the organizational stuff. I was never good at that. I had always been a very active volunteer, but the type who did what she was told, not the 'be in charge and ask others to help' type. This program is for the girls, but it's also for me. From it, I have seen that I too can do anything."

"Sometimes I look at the program like, *This is for my brother*," says Shari. "What I appreciate about running and about Girls on the Run is that I can look back now and say something good came out of his cancer. He fought long and hard and left a young family behind, but his hardship led me down this path that I am on now, and I can't imagine my life without Girls on the Run. It's become a priority."

By fall of 2005, the program had expanded to a hundred girls each year. There are now four Girls on the Run programs each fall and spring in Hailey and Ketchum, the two towns near Sun Valley

Resort. Shari has a policy of not turning any girl away, no matter what her financial situation, but it's hard these days, and every session is waitlisted.

"We get all kinds of girls in here. A lot of times, we'll have parents who say, 'I want my daughter to lose a little weight,' and when I hear that, I'm like, 'Okay, fine, whatever.' But what parents don't realize sometimes is that yes, we are teaching girls to run, but the bigger message is that we want to teach them how to find strength from within and to discover and celebrate their true self."

Shari remembers a certain fourth grader who had made it very clear that she didn't want to be there. Shari thought that at the end of the six weeks they would never see her again. But she signed up for the next session. Even in the second session, the girl was acting as if she didn't want to be there, but Shari had caught on and wasn't surprised when she signed up for yet a third session. "Every session you could see her getting more and more into her running. Her face started to light up when she ran, and her journal entries were more enthusiastic. By the end of four sessions, she was a whole new girl and a delight to be around, and she ended up placing third in our five-K. You could see the change in her when she crossed the finish line that year. She went on to do track in middle school."

As part of the program, Shari has each girl keep a journal recording how they feel after every run. She says it's fun for her and the coaches to read about the progress the girls are making. And at the end of a session, she says even the girls can see the changes in themselves when they read about how they felt over the six weeks. This fourth grader who came into the program unwillingly and ended up joining the junior high school track team is a perfect example.

□ □ □

Today in Hailey, Idaho, there's a mountain ash tree planted next to Paul's grave in the local cemetery. Even with the snow, you can see colorful Mardi Gras beads hanging from the tree limbs. Shari puts three new strands on the tree twice a year, and each one represents another mile Girls on the Run has run (three miles every session). She's been putting them there on the tree since Paul died in 2002.

During the run that ends each session, Shari and other volunteers hand out a different-colored strand of Mardi Gras beads at each kilometer as girls pass by (kilometers go faster than miles, so they give them five for extra support, instead of marking the miles). The beads are special to the girls. They know they're not only a symbol of how far they've come, but they're also a tribute to Shari's brother, whose death led her to start their program.

The girls also know that before Paul got sick, Shari had never run. In fact, she tells the girls that for a long time, there were a lot of things she never had the courage to do. For most of her life, she was trapped inside the Girl Box. When she started running, she stepped out timidly. Eventually, she got up her strength, and then she never looked back. "I remember my first ten-mile run. It was like I conquered the world. It was so huge. Looking back I can now see it was for me, but when I ran at first, I was doing it for Paul." She can honestly say to every girl who passes through the program, "I know how you feel." And they believe her.

Acknowledgments

While the last year might have been one of the most challenging years of my life, this book represents also what an amazing year it was as well. For the first time in my life, I had a chance to see that everyone in the world is connected in one way or another. There's nothing that we do that doesn't affect someone, even if it's as simple as going for a run or making a decision about what shoes to buy. Through this interconnectedness, there were many people without whom this book would not have been possible, and I would like to thank in particular the following:

I want to thank Holly, Radha, Gabriel, Pamela, Peter, Janne, Gregory, Sarah, Wendy, Norm and David, and the rest of my lovely family, who always supported my visions—no matter how crazy—of what to accomplish next. Alyson Wilson, who believed in my writing on days that I didn't. Alison Berkley, who has dished both good and bad my way—no matter what, I always learn from her and always know she will listen, even when she's talking. Ian Clampett, who was such a devoted friend and surf buddy in Los Angeles. Gregg Hedin for keeping me smiling today and hopefully tomorrow. Devin Alexander, who walked and ran with me in Los Angeles. Jessica Christensen, my best friend since I was fifteen, who always blazed the trail as an independent, free spirit. Rebecca, who will always have a special place in my life for opening her home and sharing her friends when

I needed help and didn't know how to ask for it. Patrick, who (along with Rebecca) helped guide me to Idaho and taught me I was going to be okay, that everything would fall into place as it should. Kaia, Tara, Idaho, Thia, and all my new, incredibly enthusiastic, inspirational girlfriends, who are always up for a challenge.

Liesl from Oakley and Ryan from Helly Hansen, who kept my buns warm this winter with outerwear when I made the move to Idaho. Other people who gave me gear to get me running and keep me traveling this year: Chico from Dakine; the GoLite and Timberland folks; Ilana at Nike; Alli at Smartwool and the Stanwood crew; Nancy at Burton; Hal, Guy, and Sierra at Salomon; Coley at Patagonia; Dave Schmidt at Himaya; Jaime Eschette at Teva; and Ian Anderson at Vail.

Kristin Carpenter, whose ongoing enthusiasm has always made me feel supported. Kristin Ulmer, whom I adore just because she is who she is. Chris Santacroce, who keeps me real. Sam Lightner, Jr., who was my friend through a hard time and convinced me to get an agent. Tom Price, who helped me get an agent, and Chris Gough for all of his agent advice. Mike Harrelson, who always made me smile when we chatted and showed me that the concept of a nuclear family is not dead.

Mr. Cooper and Bob Bumstead, who kept high school English entertaining. The Muilenberg family, especially Peter, who first showed me that people can follow their passions for writing and sports and combine the two for a career. David Hochman, of Mediabistro, who pushed me to reach deeper in my writing. My Mediabistro writing buddies, Litty, Jeff, Marisa, and Steve Maz, who used talking about writing as an excuse for us all to get together for lunch and procrastinate from actually writing.

All of the folks at the Coffee Grinder for listening to me go on and on about running for months and acted interested even if they would rather have been skiing.

Of course a big thank you to my very devoted and helpful interns, Jessica Ridenour and Miki Mori. Without you two, my work would have been even more daunting. To Edna, who transcribed hours of interviews. To Timur and Brad at We Know Macs, who fixed my computer when, in total Murphy's Law fashion, it blew up in the final hours of finishing this book.

My cousin Jenifer Sosienski, who put up with me rambling on for hours about all of my dreams and also took a huge leap by coming out to Idaho to live with me. It's been nice to see the world through her youthful eyes.

The people of Seal Press, who afforded me the opportunity to publish this book—especially Jill Rothenberg, who is an amazing runner and an even more amazing editor. My agent, Faye Bender, who navigates me through the sometimes-convoluted world of publishing.

Of course, my sidekick, Kailee, who in spite of looking like a mean pit bull is truly a woman's best friend and a great running partner.

Last, I want to thank all of the women runners in this book for teaching me about interconnectedness, whether intentionally or not.

Resources

Women Who Run

Asra Nomani
www.asranomani.com

Charlotte Lettis Richardson's documentary film *Run Like a Girl*
www.runlikeagirlfilm.com

Kathrine Switzer
www.kathrineswitzer.com

Kristin Armstrong's columns
www.runnersworld.com

Lornah Kiplgat
www.lornah.com

Pam Reed
www.pamreedrunner.com

Rebecca Rusch
www.rebeccarusch.com

Shanti Sosienski
www.shantisos.com

Featured Clubs, Organizations, and Companies

Girls on the Run (nonprofit running program for young girls)
www.girlsontherun.org

Hash House Harriers (boisterous worldwide running club)
www.gthhh.com

The Janes
www.thejanes.net

Lornah Kiplagat's High Altitude Training Centre
www.lornah.com

Moms in Motion
www.momsinmotion.com

New York Road Runners' Club
www.nyrr.org/nyrrc/org

See Jane Run (women's sports apparel company)
www.seejanerunsports.com

Tamalpa Runners
www.tamalparunners.org

Ultra Ladies
www.ultraladies.com

USATF
www.usatf.org

Featured Races

The Badwater Ultramarathon
www.badwater.com

The Bay to Breakers
www.baytobreakers.com

The Boston Marathon
www.bostonmarathon.org

Carlsbad 5000
www.eliteracing.com/carlsbad.html

Dallas White Rock Marathon
www.runtherock.com

The Dipsea Race
www.dipsea.org

The Hardrock Hundred Mile Endurance Run
www.run100s.com/HR

Helen Klein Ultra Classic
www.ultrarunner.net

Iditarod Trail Invitational
www.alaskaultrasport.com

Komen Race for the Cure
www.komen.org

Leading Ladies Marathon
http://leadingladiesmarathon.com

The Leadville Trail 100
www.leadvilletrail100.com

The New York Marathon
www.ingnycmarathon.org

Nike Women's Marathon
www.nike.com/nikemarathon

Peachtree Road Race 10K
www.atlantatrackclub.org

Pikes Peak Ascent & Marathon
www.pikespeakmarathon.org

Racing the Planet
http://racingtheplanet.com

The Raid
www.theraid.org

Team In Training
www.teamintraining.org

Teva Mountain Games
www.tevamountaingames.com

The Tucson Marathon
www.tucsonmarathon.com

Western States Endurance Run
www.ws100.com

Websites

American Running
www.americanrunning.org

Fast-Women
www.fast-women.com/news.html

Average Runner
www.averagerunner.com

Kevin Sayer's Ultra RunR Site
www.ultrunr.com

Marathon Guide
www.marathonguide.com

Running 4 Women
www.running4women.com

RunnerGirl
www.runnergirl.com

Running Research News
www.runningresearchnews.com

Run The Planet
www.runtheplanet.com

See Mommy Run
www.seemommyrun.com

Ultra Blog
http://ultrablog.us

Ultra Runner
www.ultrarunner.net

Ultra Running Online
www.ultrarunning.com

Women Runners
www.womenrunners.com

You Run Girl
www.yourungirl.com/index.html

Magazines

Her Sports
www.hersports.com

Running Times
www.runningtimes.com

Runner's World
www.runnersworld.com

Trail Runner
www.trailrunnermag.com

Women's Adventure
www.womensadventuremagazine.com

Running Camps

Andes Adventures Running Camp
www.andesadventures.com/runadv.htm
(310) 395-5265

Carmichael Training Camps
www.trainright.com

Craftbury Running Camps
www.craftsbury.com
(802) 586-7767

Fort Davis Fitness and Training Camp
www.fitnesscamp.org
(915) 584-0227

High Sierra Desert Mountain Ultra Training Camp
www.lisasmithbatchen.com/camps/sierra-camp.htm
(208) 787-2077

Jeff Galloway Running Retreats
www.jeffgalloway.com
(800) 200-2771

Lake Champlain Women's Running Camp
www.runvermont.org/women/index.html
(800) 880-8149

Malibu Running Camp
www.maliburunningcamp.com
(517) 371-4447

Women's Quest
www.womensquest.com
(303) 545-9295

Zap Fitness
www.zapfitness.com
(828) 295.6198

Books

A Woman's Guide to Running: Beginner to Elite
Annemarie Jutel, Women's Press, Ltd. (UK), 2001.

Girls on Track: A Parent's Guide to Inspiring Our Daughters to Achieve a Lifetime of Self-Esteem and Respect
Molly Barker, Ballantine Books, 2004.

Joan Benoit Samuelson's Running for Women
Joan Benoit Samuelson and Gloria Averbuch, Rodale Press, 1995.

Marathoning for Mortals
John Bingham, Jenny Hadfield, Rodale Books, 2003.

Moon Runner
Carolyn Marsden, Candlewick Press, 2005.

Running and Walking for Women over Forty: The Road to Sanity and Vanity
Kathrine Switzer, St. Martin's Griffin, 1999.

Run for Your Life: A Book for Beginning Women Runners
Deborah Reber, Perigee Books, 2002.

Running with Angels: The Inspiring Journey of a Woman Who Turned Personal Tragedy into Triumph over Obesity
Pamela Hansen, Shadow Mountain, 2005.

Runner's World Complete Book of Women's Running: The Best Advice to Get Started, Stay Motivated, Lose Weight, Run Injury-Free, Be Safe, and Train for Any Distance
Dagny Scott, Rodale Press, 2000.

Sole Sister
Jennifer Lin and Susan Warner, Andrews McMeel Publishing,
2006.

The Complete Book of Running for Women
Claire Cowlachik, Pocket Books, 1999.

*The Extra Mile: One Woman's Personal Journey to Ultra-Running
Greatness*
Pam Reed with Mitchell Sisskind, Imprint Books, 2006.

The Non-Runner's Marathon Trainer
David A. Whitsett, Forrest A Dolgener, Tanjala Jo Kole, McGraw-
Hill, 1998.

The Silence of Great Distance: Women Running Long
Frank Murphy, Windsprint Press, 2000.

The Ultimate Guide to Trail Running
Adam Chase and Nancy Hobbs, The Lyons Press, 2001.

The Women's Guide to Non-Competitive Running
Victoria Leff and Kristi Greene, RunnerMom Press, 2003.

*Wired to Run: The Runaholics Anaonymous Guide to Living with
Running Addiction*
Skip Skupien, Andrews McMeel Publishing, 2006.

Photo credits

Marathon Women, Kathrine Switzer photo courtesy of Kathrine Switzer, Jacqueline Hansen photo courtesy of Jacqueline Hansen

The Best Medicine, Diane Van Deren photo courtesy of Sethhughes.com/Hooked On The Outdoors

Marathon Mom, Kristin Armstrong photo courtesy of Elizabeth Kreutz Photography

Rusching Around the World, Rebecca Rusch photo courtesy of © www.thiakonig.com

The Transformation of a Runner, Janet Bowman photo courtesy of Skipix.com, LLC/Wendy Scipione

Fifty Thousand Miles and Going Strong, Shirley Mattson photo courtesy of Pamela S. Wendell

The Leader of the Pack, Sheryl Page photo courtesy of Bruce Ely © The Oregonian

Going the Distance, Pam Reed photo courtesy of Pam Reed

See Jane Run, Lori Shannon photo courtesy of Lori Shannon, See Jane Run Sports

Running Free, Asra Nomani photo courtesy of Dale Sparks/ALL-PRO Photography

A Double Life, Anita Ortiz photo courtesy of Anita Ortiz

Beating the Odds, Louise Cooper (with Marshall Ulrich) photo courtesy of Heather Ulrich, Team Stray Dogs

Renaissance Runner, Jeannie Wall photo courtesy of Jeannie Wall

Winning Isn't the Only Thing, Lornah Kiplagat photo courtesy of Pieter Langerhorst and Lornah Kiplagat

Unpacking the "Girl Box," photo of Shari and Paul Kunz courtesy of Shari Kunz

About the Author

Shanti Sosienski is a freelance writer based in Ketchum, Idaho. She grew up exploring the great outdoors around her hometowns of Eugene, Oregon, and Nelson, British Columbia. Her articles have appeared in *Men's Journal, Outside, Marie Claire, Self,* and *FHM.* Visit her on the web at www.shantisos.com.

Selected Titles from Seal Press

For more than thirty years, Seal Press has published ground-breaking books. By women. For women. Visit our website at www.sealpress.com.

Reckless: The Outrageous Lives of Nine Kick-Ass Women by Gloria Mattioni. $14.95. 1-58005-148-0. From Lisa Distefano, former *Playboy* model who captains a pirate vessel on her quest to protect sea life, to Libby Riddles, the first woman to win the legendary Iditarod, this collection of profiles explores the lives of nine women who took unconventional life paths to achieve extraordinary results.

The Risks of Sunbathing Topless: And Other Funny Stories from the Road edited by Kate Chynoweth. $15.95. 1-58005-141-3. From Kandahar to Baja to Moscow, these wry, amusing essays capture the comic essence of bad travel, and the female experience on the road.

Solo: On Her Own Adventure edited by Susan Fox Rogers. $15.95. 1-58005-137-5. An inspiring collection of travel narratives that reveal the complexities of women journeying alone.

The Unsavvy Traveler: Women's Comic Tales of Catastrophe edited by Rosemary Caperton, Anne Mathews, and Lucie Ocenas. $15.95. 1-58005-142-1. Thirty bitingly funny essays respond to the question: "What happens when trips go wrong?"

Woman's Best Friend: Women Writers on the Dogs in Their Lives edited by Megan McMorris. Foreword by Pam Houston. $14.95. 1-58005-163-4. An offbeat and poignant collection about those four-legged friends a girl can't do without.